THE MAGNA
CHARTA

Written and Illustrated by

JAMES DAUGHERTY

Library of Congress Catalog Card Number: 97-078470
ISBN   0-9643803-5-8
ISBN   978-0-9643803-5-6

Published by Beautiful Feet Books
1306 Mill Street
San Luis Obispo, CA 93401

www.bfbooks.com
800.889.1978

The Magna Charta

Contents

Prologue ❧ The Magic Island

THERE IS IN THE NORTH ATLANTIC A CERTAIN FAIR island called Britain. It was once a part of Europe till an encircling sea nine thousand years ago angrily bit through the connecting lowlands and rushed through a channel which is so narrow that at certain times and places when the air is clear one can see from shore to shore.

The sea that mourns and crashes on its coasts has cast its spell over the land and its history. Across its moors and forests the sea mist drifts grayly, shrouding strange shapes in vagueness and wonder.

Oak and beech springing from the damp earth covered the island with noble green forests where the nightingale sings. Placid rivers wind through flower-strewn meadows gently to the sea. Briefly the sun shines through the misty air, touching the hills and the drifting cloud rack with gold. Then again the fog rolls in, veiling the dripping forests and the lush green land with mystery and awe.

Before the time of recorded history the Druid priests raised great stones in a mystic circle to the sun and stars on lonely moors and stained their altars with human blood in dreadful sacrifices.

Ancient legends tell of how on moonlight nights King Arthur and his knights in shining mail rode through the forest glades where Oberon and Titania held their fairy court and brown Puck lurked grinning among the ferns. On stormy nights the old Norse goblins rode their demon horses down the screaming gale.

Here the white unicorn with golden horn browsed on the flower-strewn grass and lovely Una with her guardian lion shunned the scaly dragon breathing flame. Here men have heard unearthly music and woven legends into measured rhythms and here great poets have sung immortal songs.

Ever since the dim ages when restless tribes first wandered across Europe, men have coveted this island paradise with a deep desire. For hundreds of years the invaders, wave upon plundering wave, swept down upon her low-lying shores and, sailing up her rivers, drove deep into the heart of the land, slaying and burning. Celt and Briton, Pict and Roman, Saxon and Viking, Dane and Norman landed and ravaged and settled in the land through long centuries.

Gradually these people, conquerors and conquered, mingled and became one race and the mixture is richer for what each has brought.

In spite of wars and cruel oppressions there has always remained an unquenchable love of liberty and justice in the heart of this race.

Because of this, in the course of centuries, slowly with long delays and many reverses yet persistent and enduring, this people has framed a way of government which has made and kept them the freest people on earth.

When these restless children of the Northmen and Vikings perilously crossed the western sea and peopled the continental wilderness of North America they brought with them their precious heritage of freedom.

When danger to these rights and liberties threaten us from without or from within we, the English-speaking people, remember our hard-won heritage of freedom and stand together dauntless and unsubdued until the victory is won and the storm is past.

Twice in our century has this, our heritage, been in deadly peril and has been preserved at untold cost.

When we know the story of how our liberties were won and at what price, we will value and guard them, for they are not ours alone. They bear no national label—they belong to all Mankind.

WILLIAM
The Conqueror
b.1027 d.1087
MARRIED MATILDA
OF FLANDERS

|

HENRY I
b.1068 d.1135
MARRIED MATILDA
OF SCOTLAND

|

Matilda
d.1167
MARRIED GEOFFREY,
COUNT OF ANJOU

|

HENRY II
b.1133 d.1189
MARRIED ELEANOR
OF AQUITAINE

|

Henry	RICHARD I	Geoffrey	JOHN
b.1155 d.1183	b.1157 d.1199	b.1158 d.1186	b.1167 d.1216

Geoffrey
MARRIED CONSTANCE,
HEIRESS OF BRITTANY

|

Arthur,
DUKE OF BRITTANY
d.1187

PART ONE ❧
THE TWELFTH
CENTURY

Living in the Twelfth Century

IF YOU WERE LIVING IN THE TWELFTH CENTURY IN England you would be somebody's vassal. Nearly everybody in the twelfth century was someone's vassal.

The king and the bishops were the Pope's vassals.

The barons and even many bishops were the king's vassals.

The knights were the baron's vassals.

[6]

The farmers were the knight's tenants, and the laborers or villeins, as they were called, were the vassals of practically everybody.

In particular you would be the vassal of your lord, the baron on whose estate you lived and worked. You would have a special occupation with special duties. And as such you would have certain rights and privileges, but you would never have heard of freedom of speech, freedom of religion, freedom from want or freedom from fear. You could not leave your baron's estate without his permission.

Very probably you would not know how to read or write.

You would pay without question whatever taxes your king, your baron and your church demanded. For a misdemeanor or for disobedience you would be tried, sentenced and punished by your lord solely according to his will. The punishment might be ear cropping, tongue slitting or a hand or foot cut off. If you had been a leader in stirring up any sort of rebellion you would most certainly be hanged. If you refused to confess to the charges brought against you, you could be tortured horribly until you did so.

One of your privileges would be protection. In the private wars which your lord carried on perpetually with his neighbors and in which you were called on without notice to fight, you would have the privilege of fleeing to your lord's castle while his enemies burned your house, cut down your orchard, drove off your cattle and defiled your well.

This system of vassalage was called "feudal." It was a great improvement on the violence and disorder of previous ages. It was a snug and complete society in which everyone had his place in a sort of pyramid in which each was dependent on and subject to another. It was maintained by force rather than law. The greatest crime was disloyalty, treason or disobedience to your lord.

The system was considered so perfect that change or progress was never even dreamed of. If you were loyal to your king, your bishop and your lord, life could be, if not exactly beautiful, at least endurable. In the upper classes a certain amount of quarreling and fighting was allowable without the system's being upset. The king, the Church and the barons were almost continually quarreling over the powers and rights of each. This triangular warfare became so ruthless that the Church and the barons were finally able to force the king to sign a charter by which certain rights were established for every class and individual in the nation. This charter is called the Magna Charta.

Although the quarreling between the king, the barons and the Church continued under the feudal system for centuries, the Magna Charta remained the basis upon which equal rights were established and maintained by law.

The foregoing is not an exact or complete account of the feudal system, which was amazingly complex, but it includes some of the ideas you would have been used to if you lived in the twelfth century, and some of the conditions out of which much of our present system evolved and grew. Many of our ideas today are modified remnants of the feudal system.

If you were a young man living in the latter half of the twelfth century, you would often be following your lord to war with or against King John in England and France. And you would be taking part in and talking about many of the events that happened in the following true story.

Castles and Cathedrals

ON THE HIGH SPOTS OF ENGLAND, THE DOMINANT hills that overlooked wide valleys, William the Conqueror had built his castles. Their crenelated walls and turrets and high donjon keeps rose nobly against the sky, for the Normans were builders whose masons laid stone on stone to last through the centuries.

Each castle defended a wide domain or "fief" which the Conqueror had given to a trusted noble to hold in perpetuity as long as he furnished on call a specified number of knights and men-at-arms for the king's army. If the noble failed to do this, he would forfeit his lands to the crown. To possess his lands, the noble knelt before the king and swore fealty or loyalty to his lord.

On the same terms of loyalty and service sub-tenants held land from their lord or his knights. These farmers, called yeomen, and laborers, called villeins, worked two or three days each week on the lands of their lord besides tilling their own allotted fields. In addition, they were required to pay numerous taxes, fines and fees which were continually assessed by king, baron and Church to keep this fine show going. These dues were paid mostly in goods and services, for there was little money in circulation.

The king caused all the rich and powerful among his subjects to take an oath of loyalty and service to him. So besides being the largest landowner, the king had on call the most powerful army in England.

Over this scene of splendor, cruelty and degradation swept war, famine and pestilence, taking toll of high and low alike.

In the great hall of his castle, the baron was supreme ruler of his domain. Here he settled quarrels, administered what passed for justice, received his rents and fines from his tenants, and planned assaults on his neighboring barons.

The castle was a self-sustaining unit, a busy place

of comings and goings, swarming with servants, soldiers and guests. If it happened to be a feast day, which was often, the savory odors of roasting and baking greeted the noses of hungry guests and penetrated everywhere.

Much preparation went into the making of a successful feast day. Indeed, it began on the day before, at dawn, when the baron and all his retinue had ridden gaily to the forest for the hunt. There was shouting, barking of hounds, and the sweet notes of the hunting horn. For the pack had picked up the scent of a wild boar and rushed baying among the ancient oaks and beeches of the forest. The hunt was on.

By late afternoon the baron had outridden his scattered retinue and alone had come upon the great boar at bay between the roots of fallen trees. Red-eyed and foaming, the savage monster held off the baying pack. Several of the baron's favorite hounds lay torn and mangled. As the baron dismounted and came forward, the foaming beast charged at him. Bracing himself behind his heavy boar spear, the baron drove it through the animal's heart. In answer to his winding horn his scattered followers soon found him. With loud admiration of his skill and valor, the gay cavalcade rode back to the castle hungry and weary.

All next day the kitchens were busy with preparation. That night in the great hall of the donjon a huge log burned merrily on the hearth. In the murky light of smoking torches, bright banners and rich tapestries gleamed on the walls. On a dais at the head of the hall the baron and his lady amid his knights and noble guests sat at table. High-born ladies, gorgeous in silken gowns of red and blue, exchanged smiles and coarse jests with curly-haired young squires in striped hose and embroidered doublets with enormous scalloped sleeves. In the lower hall at trestled tables on backless benches sprawled the lesser folk— men-at-arms, hostlers, foresters, farmers, tenants with their broad-hipped wives, pilgrims, peddlers and wandering friars.

Scullions now brought in the smoking boar's head to the baron's table amid loud applause. Other dishes were passed about—roast fowl, huge cheeses, bread and puddings. Hungry guzzlers filled their wooden plates with ample helpings again and again.

Rare wines circulated at the nobles' table and among the baser born great flagons of ale and cider were filled and emptied repeatedly. Under and even on the tables various breeds of unhousebroken dogs and pups mingled freely in the festivities. Later on, lean cats and armies of rude and lusty rats found their share among the bones and scraps strewn on the rush-covered floor. Dogs, cats and rats carried on a private warfare of their own.

During the feasting a minstrel rose and strummed his lute, reciting the song of Tristan and Isolde. In pauses of the song jugglers came forward and performed their feats. At the lower tables travelers told fantastic tales of strange lands, and a friar recounted how in a dream the devil had carried him through the horrors of purgatory and hell itself and how he had been rescued from roasting by a holy saint and brought safely back to earth.

When the night grew late straw mattresses were brought in and flung on the vermin-infested floor. On these the whole company stretched out with their clothes on and soon a symphony of snores rose thunderously as the flickering torches went out one by one. All but the sentries slept.

Towers other than those of castles were rising skyward above the green English countryside. These were the gray stone cathedrals of the Church, carved and lacelike. Their slender columns reached toward the heavens in lovely fanlike pointed arches. Through their great rose windows the light fell softly in rainbow hues. On the sculptured facade tall angels and saints in stone smiled with a mysterious tenderness and carved figures told the stories of the Bible to unlettered worshipers, for the Church was the father and mother of the poor.

The Church was more potent than king or barons for it ruled the hearts and souls of men. To it every Christian must pay a tenth, or tithe, of his produce or earnings. Sufficient to itself, the Church owned and managed vast estates for which its bishops did homage and paid taxes to the king. In its monasteries and abbeys, pious scholars found refuge and peace from a world of violence and cruelty. Here artist-scholars copied the sacred writings on parchment pages which they illumined with glowing designs of red and blue and gold. At the gates, monks dispensed daily bread to the hungry, poor and maimed, of whom there were plenty. Archbishops and bishops took part with the barons in the councils and courts of the king where some, because of their wisdom and virtue, guided and strengthened the kingdom in times of danger and distress.

In the quiet cloisters and scriptoriums of their monasteries, scholarly monks labored patiently on their chronicles. These documents sometimes began with the creation of the world, continued with the history of the Greeks and Romans, and were brought up to date. They were added to year by year with the recordings of current events. As the clergy were in close touch with what went on at the court and councils of the king and knew personally many of the most important people, the latest entries in the chronicles were apt to be a lively and accurate record of the day's events. This factual matter was sprinkled with terrifying accounts of the doings of the devil. A very active person at all times in human affairs, he was usually overcome by the saintly activities of holy bishops who, by their miracles and healings, greatly discomfited his satanic majesty.

Underneath all and close bound to the earth in this feudal world were the serfs and villeins, the base born, half-slave drudges whose unending labor built the castles and cathedrals and who, in goods and services, paid the fines, fees and taxes laid unceasingly by king and baron and bishop on the patient and enduring backs of the English people.

A peasant's house was a thatched, one-room hovel made of mud and wattles. Cooking was done over an open fire. There being no chimney, a hole in the roof let out some of the smoke. It also let out most of the heat. The whole family slept in their clothes in a single featherbed or on straw pallets on the floor. Soap, baths, plumbing, doctors and dentists were unknown.

If, after taxes, their barns were still half full and there was meat in the pot, then life was good and there was dancing on the village green.

But with the vast patience and endurance of the common people these peasants raised their crops, tended their cattle and, when they prospered, thanked the good saints.

HENRY II

PART TWO ❧
THE ANGEVINS

The Laughable Adventure of the Irishmen's Whiskers

JOHANS SANZ TERRE — JOHN LACKLAND, EVERYONE called him.

It was a nickname his father, King Henry II, had given him at his christening and the name had stuck.

King Henry had plenty of land to give away on both sides of the English Channel, for his dominions reached from Scotland to the Pyrenees. But there had been three sons, Henry, Geoffrey and Richard before John, and the King had done handsomely by each one. When John arrived on Christmas Eve, 1167, there was not much land left and so his father had given him an extra measure of his affection and made him his favorite of all the royal children. This love deepened when his eldest son Henry died at an early age, leaving as successors to the throne Richard, Geoffrey and John, in that order.

When John was only nine years old, King Henry proclaimed him King of Ireland, or that part of it which the English had conquered.

John was a bright boy and was spoiled by his mother, Queen Eleanor of Aquitaine, and the court.

As he grew he picked up their fine Norman manners and graceful turn of speech. Listening to the gossip and politics that boiled around him, he took on too easily the Norman guile and greed, and the cruelty and unscrupulousness of the fierce party factions that schemed and struggled for power. He was fond of reading and liked fine clothes.

When he became twenty-one his father made him a knight and ordered him to visit Ireland. For this pleasant assignment young John gathered his favorite companions together with about three hundred knights and a large number of archers and yeomen and marched gaily across England in the lovely April weather. Sixty ships carried them across the channel to Ireland.

Shortly after their landing, a delegation of shaggy Irish chieftains came to pay homage to their new overlord. John and his knights were very amused at the wild appearance of his barbaric subjects and laughed heartily in their faces. When the chieftains knelt to swear allegiance the new overlord could not resist pulling and tweaking their long curly beards and laughing even louder. This is never a safe thing to do to an Irishman.

Boiling with rage, the chiefs leaped up and departed, swearing vengeance for the insult. The Irish uprising that followed would have been excuse enough to send John and his friends hurrying home. As it happened, however, there was another reason as well. The King sent word that John's elder brother, Geoffrey, had died. This made John second in succession to the throne, and he was ordered to return home at once.

King Henry II was the great grandson of William the Conqueror, and because he was Count of Anjou as well, his family were called Angevins. They were a restless, quarrelsome, turbulent family and they gave the old king a great deal of trouble. When wives were troublesome, their husbands sometimes kept them in prison. Henry's Queen Eleanor was placed in enforced seclusion for sixteen years. His sons were continually fighting with each other and quarreling with their harassed parent. Nor was that all. Richard, heir to the throne, formed an alliance with the King of France. When Henry with his army attempted to punish his son he was beaten so badly that he was compelled to sue for peace on Richard's own terms.

It was a bitter blow and the old King lay sick and heartbroken on his death bed. A list of those besides Richard who had turned traitor was brought to him. Lifting himself heavily on his elbow, he said feebly, "Read . . . read."

"By your leave, not now, Sire," said the retainer hesitantly.

"Read, man, read," groaned the King.

"Sire, the first name written down here is that of Lord John, your son."

How King Richard Was Crowned and Went Upon the Third Crusade

In all the pomp and splendor of his coronation Richard himself was the most splendid figure of all. He was tall, a powerful figure of a man, a born soldier, the perfect knight and a fearless leader of men.

His younger brother John marched in the procession of nobles and bishops preceding the King to the altar. He carried one of the three splendid swords of justice with the golden scabbards from the King's treasury. John took in all the details of the ceremony with interest, thinking of how he himself would act if and when his turn came.

After the coronation, the King took off his royal regalia and feasted and drank with his nobles till the wine overflowed the tables.

The nobles who guarded the King had noticed Jews among the crowd in the church. This was contrary to the King's command as they were believed to cast evil spells at such times. These Jews were arrested, scourged and their property was confiscated.

London mobs, encouraged by this example, plundered and burned the houses of the Jews, massacring men and women. Those who escaped took refuge in the Tower of London, where they were under the protection of the King. The hysteria of hate spread from town to town throughout the country. Everywhere Jews were slaughtered and their houses pillaged and burned.

Although these robberies and massacres were popularly regarded as acts of piety, such acts were contrary to custom, for the Jews were under the protection of the king. In fact, they were one of his chief sources of revenue. Extracting money from the Jews by torture if necessary was a royal privilege reserved for the king alone. Richard decreed that there should be no more persecutions.

When news came from the Holy Land that the Third Crusade against the Saracens was not going too well, Richard received an invitation from Philip of France to join him in the Crusade and go to Jerusalem. Richard accepted with enthusiasm. The Church was urging all true Christians to "take the cross"—that is, to join the Crusade. As an inducement the Pope absolved the souls of all who did so. Even the legal debts of the Crusaders were canceled. The Crusade offered knightly adventure in strange lands, as well as an escape from the boredom of castle life. Young knights and old donned their chain mail and eagerly rode to the King's standard to rescue the Holy Sepulcher from the hands of the Saracens.

Richard began raising funds at once. He put up for sale lordships, townships, castles, woods, farms and charters. The King's sheriffs and their officers were compelled to pay fines to retain their offices and a tax of the tenth part of all movable possessions was generally levied throughout England. The taxpayers groaned and paid but sighed with relief when the last of the Crusaders left England for the Holy Land. The Crusades were an expensive luxury for the taxpayer.

Of How John Tarried in England and of Richard's Return

JOHN STRETCHED HIS SHORT MUSCULAR BODY AND yawned. He was not interested in crusades. In fact, they bored him. Now that big brother Richard was away he felt freer. The farther Richard was from England, the closer John felt to the throne. The

King had generously given him six counties and more castles for which he was accountable to no one. He was also Lord of Ireland. This was a promising start for his plans to take over the kingdom in his brother's absence.

John was very pleased when some of the most powerful bishops and barons held a council and expelled John's most powerful enemy, William of Longchamps, who represented the authority of the King in his absence.

But there were true and loyal men in England who would guard and defend her with their lives. There always have been such who have stood by their country in her darkest hours. Of these, two were among the most powerful men in England: William Marshal and Hubert Walter. The latter was the most saintly and venerated bishop in England. In the King's absence the two men kept watch against his enemies, for there were many of these, both at home and abroad.

Meanwhile, troubadours and ballad singers were spreading Richard's fame and news of his exploits in the Holy Land across Europe. All people hailed him as the perfect knight, the hero king, the champion of Christendom.

Actually, things were not going well with Richard. Money was giving out. The plague was ravaging his troops and Saladin, the Saracen prince, had held Jerusalem against all comers. Richard's ally, Philip of France, had grown jealous and quarrelsome and had sourly returned to France where, indeed, he had belonged all the time. The Crusaders returned to their ships and sailed for home.

Richard's ship encountered storms and he disembarked at the nearest port and started on the long, overland journey across Europe. It was a perilous one for Richard, for if captured, he would be a valuable prize worth a huge ransom. It was the Duke of Austria who captured this valuable prize and promptly sold him to the German Emperor for a handsome price.

Meanwhile, the news had come to England that Richard was returning from the Holy Land, but where he was or even if he were alive was not known. There were rumors that he was a captive in one of the Duke of Austria's castles.

At this John's hopes rose. It seemed that all his plans were working out. King Philip of France had returned from the Holy Land and sent an invitation to John to come over and see what they could arrange now that Richard was out of the way. They agreed that neither would make a separate peace with Richard in case he should appear. They also agreed that when John became King of England Philip would give him most of Normandy and all the Angevin lands of his ancestors, in return for which John would acknowledge fealty to Philip.

John returned to England with the sad news that his dear brother was dead—or so he said. He arrogantly demanded of the great council the kingdom and the allegiance of the nobles and the people.

The justiciars (they were the officers who represented the authority of the absent King) denounced John's statement and demand as a lie and a bald-faced act of treason. Nevertheless John fortified his English castles and incited the Welsh to rebel, which they were always glad to do. He also called on Philip for aid, and the French King assembled an invasion fleet to send across the Channel.

The justiciars met this threat with so powerful an army of defense that John's castles were besieged and several taken and the threatened French invasion was abandoned.

News at last reached England from Richard in his Austrian prison. He ordered that his ransom be collected—the staggering sum of 940 pounds in silver.

In order to enlist John in collecting the ransom, the barons made a truce with him by which his castles were restored to him and he in turn agreed under oath to raise part of the ransom from his own estates.

Richard had already cost his people plenty in blood and treasure; now they must pay again to buy back their absentee king. But so strict was the feudal obligation to ransom an overlord that noble and bishop and serf again paid taxes and gave gifts for this purpose without protest.

"All bishops, priests, earls and barons, abbacies and priories were assessed one quarter of their income and moreover they gave their gold and silver vessels for that work of piety." The great ransom treasure grew daily. When more than half was collected it was sent in bulk to the German Emperor together with hostages who were to be held until the rest of the ransom had been paid.

John watched all this with increasing anxiety. Nor did he feel any better when he received a brief message from the King of France. He turned pale as he read, "Take care of yourself, the devil is loosed." He knew this meant that Richard had been released by the German Emperor.

John hurried over to France where he and Philip made a last bid to prevent Richard's return. They sent the German Emperor an offer of one hundred and fifty thousand marks if he would detain Richard a year or deliver him into their hands. The Emperor smiled broadly as he showed this letter to his royal prisoner, but he wisely decided to take the English ransom money ready at hand rather than to trust Lord John's and the French King's offer.

All London turned out with banners and trumpets

to give Richard the Lion-Hearted a royal welcome as he rode into the city proud and magnificent on his great charger. All of the rebel castles with the exception of Nottingham had fallen into the hands of loyal Hubert Walter. When Richard appeared before its walls this castle surrendered also and all England was his.

Richard now held a council which cited John to appear for trial within forty days on the charge of treason.

John quietly departed for France and when the forty days were up Richard crossed over to settle accounts with King Philip. He held no resentment against his treacherous brother. One of John's friends at the King's court brought him a message saying, "You are in luck's way. The King is simple and pitiful, and kinder to you than you would have been to him. Come, the King awaits you."

John went to Richard at once. As the door opened behind him, Richard rose and turned. John stood bowed in the doorway for a moment and then threw himself on the floor at Richard's feet, weeping hysterically. The King stooped and lifted him to his feet. Visibly moved, he kissed John and said, "Think no more of it. You were but a child and left to ill guardians. Evil were their thoughts who counseled you amiss." Presently he added gaily, "Come, let us eat. I have a fine salmon freshly caught to cheer you."

The Treasure of Châlus

It WAS TRUE THAT A GOODLY TREASURE LAY IN THE
donjon keep of Castle Châlus. This had given rise to
a marvelous tale that had gone through Normandy
and everyone believed it to be absolutely true. It was
said that in Châlus twelve golden knights sat about a
golden table heaped with dazzling jewels. Richard
was not the man to doubt it or to forego such a prize,
and so he and his goodly array laid siege day and
night under the walls of the castle of Châlus.

One day, in the corner tower of the castle's outer wall, two archers peered out through a narrow slit. Below they could see the King as he rode around the walls in his daily tour of inspection and defiance.

" 'Twould be a wondrous fair target if any harquebus in the whole world were strong enow to carry thus far," mused one of the archers named Jehan.

His companion, Pierre, a short powerful man, was slowly turning the creaking windlass of his harquebus and the metal bow was slowly bending under the relentless pull. "Well," he muttered, "we will let my crossbow, 'Spitfire Blanche,' throw him an iron kiss for luck."

Pierre rested the heavy weapon on the ledge of the aperture and sighted carefully. He pulled the trigger and the bow discharged with an angry snarl. Far below the horseman jerked backward and, as his horse reared, fell to the ground.

"By Saint Sebastian, a hit, a hit!" yelled Jehan. "Thou hast brought down the noblest knight in Christendom," he cried, pounding Pierre's back with his fist.

For ten days King Richard, mortally wounded, lay bearing his agony with knightly fortitude as the great stone-throwing machines breached the walls of Châlus and the English pikemen fought their way into the castle foot by foot. Taken at last, the castle yielded some treasure, but the twelve marvelous golden knights were found to be merely a delusion.

Richard had followed many golden illusions and he had pursued them vainly through rivers of blood. The violent deeds and generous impulses of his nature had earned him the nickname "Richard Yea and Nay." As he lay on his pallet he knew that he was surrendering to the last enemy left to him—Death. But there was time yet for one more generous impulse. When the archer who had mortally wounded him was brought to him for judgment he smiled faintly and said, "Ha, let him go free!"

PART THREE
KING JOHN AND
THE MAGNA CHARTA

Of How John Was Made King 1199

WILLIAM MARSHAL HAD COME LATE AT NIGHT TO rouse Archbishop Hubert Walter with news that could not wait till morning. Richard was dead. Briefly the story was told. The two men sat silent for a while as the yellow candlelight etched their stern faces against the darkness of their surroundings.

William was the first to break the silence, coming at once to the point. "My lord," he said, "we must hasten to choose someone whom we may make king."

After a long pause the Archbishop said slowly, "I think and believe that we ought to make Arthur king. As the son of Geoffrey, he stands nearest to the throne, by right and by birth."

William Marshal frowned and shook his head. "To my way of thinking that would be bad. He is only a boy, counseled by traitors, and by nature haughty and proud. If we set him over us he will seek evil against us, for he loves not the people of this land. He shall not come here yet by my advice. Look rather to Count John. My conscience and my knowledge point him out to me as the nearest heir to the land which was his father's and his brother's."

The Archbishop leaned forward in his chair and,

JOHN
LACKLAND

speaking earnestly, said slowly, "Marshal, is this really your desire?"

"Yea, my lord, for it is reason. Unquestionably, a son has nearer claim to his father's land than a grandson. It is right that he should have it."

The Archbishop was a man of few words. "So be it then," he said. "But mark well my words, Marshal: Of nothing else that ever you did in your life will you have so much cause to repent as of what you are doing now."

"I thank you," answered William, bowing his head. Then, rising, he added, "Nevertheless, I deem that this is as it should be."

Both men knew well enough the foulness of John's character. But to Marshal it seemed that to make Arthur king would be to deliver England into the hands of Philip of France. For the boy was in Philip's care and had grown up under the French King's influence.

It was a choice between two dangerous courses but none knew better than Marshal that it was no time to deliver the kingdom into the hands of a boy who was a weakling. Wicked as he knew John to be, he also knew that John was capable, crafty and experienced and would staunchly defend what was his own.

John came eagerly across the water to London to receive his kingdom from the royal council which with one accord had acclaimed him their king. Solemnly he swore the triple oath, to love and to preserve the holy Church and its ordained priests, to do away with all bad laws and to establish good ones, and to see justice done throughout all England. Then Hubert Walter, Archbishop of Canterbury, placed the jeweled crown of England on his head. From the great throng of nobles and bishops rose the clamorous shout, "Long live the king!"

After the coronation John was busy with the affairs of England, but his thoughts were centered on Normandy and the French provinces that had been his father's. Now that he was king he would make sure of these dominions against Philip of France.

In a few days he was again in Normandy. Here the Duke of Flanders came and made an alliance with him. Afterward he met in a snarling conference with Philip and the two renewed their old quarrels, for Philip demanded the French provinces for Prince Arthur, who was John's nephew. Soon the two kings were at war playing the old game of taking each other's castles.

ELEANOR of AQUITANE

A Great Lady 1202

ELEANOR OF AQUITAINE WAS THE GREAT LADY OF HER
age. She was the only woman who had ever been
queen both of France and England. She was the
mother of two kings of England, and two of her
daughters became queens by marriage.

In all her stormy eighty years she had seen many
battles and sieges and experienced desperate perils. As
she looked grimly down from the only tower of her
Castle of Mirebeau that had not been taken, she
swore she would never surrender it. The breached
walls, the outer ward and all the gates save one were
in the hands of her enemies. Her own grandson, the
twelve-year-old Arthur of Brittany, aided by Philip
and the nobles of Poitou, had laid siege to the castle
and finally driven Eleanor and her few retainers into
the last tower. She had sent a letter calling on her
son King John at Le Mans, eighty miles away, to come
to her rescue. Two days had passed and no word had
come. Anxiously now she watched the white road that
wound over the hills to the horizon.

All at once a cloud of dust could be seen in the
distance, followed by the glint of light on metal. A
long column of cavalry was advancing rapidly over
the hills. It was King John and his knights, coming
to the rescue! Below in the castle ward rose the

clamor of trumpet blasts and horsemen mounting as the besiegers sallied out to meet the surprise attack. The two charging hosts met head on, surging forward and back in a melee of wild confusion. But the tide of battle pushed inward as King John's knights pressed forward crying, "A rescue, a rescue!"

Both the defenders and attackers were carried within the gates by the furious onrush of the assault, and the battle raged on within the walls. In an hour the castle was taken. There was rich booty, for many nobles of Poitou and Anjou, and two hundred knights, were taken prisoner to be held for ransom. Prince Arthur himself was among those captured.

The prisoners were chained and sent to damp dungeons to await liberation by ransom.

"Ah, my son, my son," cried the old Queen through her tears to John, "I knew you would not fail me. God hath wrought for us a glorious victory and overthrown our enemies by His mighty arm."

What to do with his nephew Arthur was a very serious problem for John, for the boy boldly claimed the throne of England and the whole Angevin dominions as Richard's lawful heir.

John's advisers proposed a solution that would remove the danger. "Put out the boy's eyes," they suggested. It would be momentarily painful but not fatal, they pointed out, and would be entirely effective in removing Arthur as an active threat to his uncle's throne. John agreed to this plan and sent three experienced retainers to execute it. John's executioners were not squeamish men but when it actually came to touching the hot iron to the young Prince's eyes they refused.

However, word was sent to the King that the order had been carried out and that Arthur had died from the ordeal. When this rumor reached the nobles of Brittany they threatened vengeance and immediate war. This was prevented only by the confession of the King's executioners that Arthur was still alive and unharmed.

Thinking that his nephew might now listen to reason, King John called Arthur before him. He wished to befriend and honor him, he said gently,

and would do so if Arthur would forsake the evil company of the French and their king and adhere to his loving uncle and lord. The boy, facing the grim circle of his enemies, arrogantly demanded that John surrender the kingdom of England and the Angevin domains. He himself was the heir of King Richard and by hereditary right all these lands were his. If John would not do this immediately there would be no peace between them, he said. Certainly the boy had inherited the family pride and his Uncle Richard's lion-hearted courage, if not his kingdom.

For a few moments John, checking his wrath, bit his lip and drummed on his chair with his fingers. The boy gave him no choice. He would have to do away with him.

"Send him to Rouen and imprison him there in the new tower under close guard," John ordered.

After the iron doors of the new tower had closed on the young Prince he was never seen again. But heaps of human bones sometimes found in the dungeon keeps of medieval castles told grim stories. Of them all, an ugly rumor repeated by John's enemies was the worst. It was said that in a drunken rage he had murdered his nephew with his own hands. Though there is no actual proof of this story, it came to be generally believed throughout all Europe.

The Sheriff of Nottingham and the Men in Lincoln Green

THE SHERIFF OF NOTTINGHAM WAS A MAN WITH A keen eye and a sharp nose whose profitable and unpopular duty it was to collect the king's taxes, rents, fines and numerous other items that contributed to the royal income.

The sheriff was diligent in his office and when he espied a fat pig, a goodly team of oxen or even a comely farmer's daughter, he seized upon them in the king's name and for the defense of the realm. Anyone who protested his action, whether it was the Earl of Huntingdon or a common swineherd, was promptly outlawed.

Beyond the walls of Nottingham stretched ancient Sherwood Forest. Here, an outlawed Saxon who was agile enough to escape the sheriff's officers might find refuge from the king's hangman.

The outlaws of Sherwood Forest were sometimes called "the Merry Men in Lincoln Green," for they wore green doublets, hunted the king's deer, defied the sheriff, robbed the rich who came riding through the forest, and shared their loot with peasants stripped bare by the tax gatherers. Their leader was renowned throughout the countryside by the name of Robin Hood.

Many a Norman merchant passing with his pack train through the forest toward the next market town trembled and clutched his purse when he heard a winding horn answered again and again down the forest aisles.

For presently, a lithe young man in a green doublet would step from the underbrush, followed by a blond Saxon giant with a huge quarterstaff. With him would be a paunchy friar, his tucked-up cassock displaying an enormous pair of hairy legs. Be-

ROBIN HOOD

hind every tree stood a green archer with drawn bowstring.

"I am called Robin Hood, at your service," the young man would say gaily, lifting his cap, "and these are my companions, Little John and the holy Friar Tuck. The rest are the Merry Men of Sherwood Forest. We have come to your aid to lighten your burdens."

After a brief scuffle in which Little John rapped several of the sheriff's henchmen roundly on the pate, the Merry Men would drive off the pack mules with their burdens of merchandise. Meanwhile, the merchants were hauled off their mules and the Friar stripped them of their heavy money belts, saying merrily, "The love of money is the root of all evil."

"Carry our greetings to the Sheriff of Nottingham and all other such Norman robbers," Robin would call. "Say we do welcome them to the forest that they may take our taxes to King John."

The ballad of Robin Hood and his Merry Men was handed down by stubborn Saxon peasants, men who in their hearts loved liberty, and by restless individualists and disturbers of the peace who troubled the dreams of comfortable people who wanted to keep things the way they always had been.

Such a rebel was one William of the Long Beard who later on preached that the poor of London should have more of the good things of life. When the king's officers came for him, he took sanctuary in the church tower of St. Mary le Bow. But he was smoked out and hanged on the king's gibbet with nine of his followers as a warning to troublemakers.

There were quieter ways to achieve justice and right. They took longer, but they were less violent. As straggling villages grew into prosperous towns, merchants began to grow rich and formed themselves into "guilds" or companies for their mutual protection and interest. As the guilds in these towns grew richer, they petitioned the king for exemptions from labor service on their lords' lands, for the right to elect their own mayor and councilmen and to hold public meetings to act on town affairs. If the king needed money, which was nearly always the case, he sometimes granted these privileges for a good round sum. The town was then given a charter with the royal seal stating what rights and privileges the king had granted it. The towns which had these charters valued and guarded them, for they secured the liberties of the people.

Thus through the years and centuries the people of the English towns quietly bought their freedoms bit by bit. In times of oppression and violence, the people of the towns stubbornly claimed their rights, saying to the tyrants and persecutors, "See, here are our liberties granted in our charter bearing the king's own seal."

[49]

Of How King John Lost His Lands Across the Water

IN THESE DAYS TALES OF MIRACLES AND WONDERS were common gossip repeated by peasants, priests and nobles alike, and King John always gave them his serious attention. Just before Christmas in the year 1200, reliable reports were circulated that four moons had been seen in the four quarters of the heavens. "A fifth had appeared in the middle of the first four, with several stars around it; and this last one with its accompanying stars made the circuit of the other four moons five times or more. This phenomenon lasted for about an hour, to the wonder of many who beheld it."

John never doubted such stories for a moment, for to him they portended that remarkable events and dreadful disasters were about to occur. But none of his councilors could forecast just what these would be. John hoped very much that they would all happen to the King of France, for though John had beaten him badly at Mirebeau, Philip had elsewhere continued to capture his castles with unbroken success.

However, John was very happy for he had just married a lovely, twelve-year-old girl named Isabella of Angoulême. His first wife, Hawisa (or Avisa), was called Isabella of Gloucester, for she was the daughter of the Earl of Gloucester, and was his second cousin. This had troubled his conscience ever since he had seen Isabella of Angoulême, and on these grounds he had divorced Hawisa.

On account of Philip's successes, many Norman nobles were going over to the French King, and even John's bull-necked English barons were getting restless at his inaction. They began to call him "Softsword" behind his back, and finally many of them who had followed him to Normandy went home to England where they said they rightfully belonged. Here they reported that John had been bewitched by sorcery from attacking Philip. To all this John merely laughed and said, "Let him alone. Whatever Philip now seizes, I will one day recover."

Suddenly John was awakened from his pleasant dreams by the unhappy discovery that he was running out of money and supplies, and that he no longer had means or men to defend his Angevin dominions.

THE ANGEVIN TEMPER

A Call to Arms 1205

When the Angevins became angry, and this was very often, they would go into fits of very bad temper. When King John was angry, he threw himself down and rolled on the floor, yelling and chewing the expensive oriental rugs that Crusaders had brought back from the East. If there were no rugs about, he chewed the straw and sticks that littered the floor. It was bad for his teeth. At such times the dogs, servants, and hostages fled from the palace and the nobles left town.

The King had come back from Normandy in one of his usual rages. It was all the fault of those traitors, the barons, he said. They had deserted him in the midst of his enemies. This was true. Those who held estates in the provinces of France would not take sides with John, for they were bound by their oath of fealty to the King of France; and if they fought against him, he would confiscate their estates.

Worst of all, John had no money and because of this he was, for the moment, powerless. But soon his fighting spirit was aroused. So the barons had called him "Softsword"! He would show them otherwise. He levied a tax of one-seventh of all movable goods on the whole kingdom—barons, bishops, and commoners. A high tax of this sort amounted almost to confiscation, but in time the King's sheriffs were able to collect most of it.

Following this, John summoned the nobles to a council. He announced that the kingdom was in danger of invasion by the King of France. Supplies for the army must be raised at once. John decreed that those who would not take active part could instead pay a fine of two and a half marks, called "scutage." The cowed barons granted all this.

As money began to pour into the royal treasury again, the King felt better. But the danger was not really past. He could trust no one. His nobles might be plotting even now to go over to Philip. He would find out when he called out the army to defend the kingdom.

He was determined to win back the French provinces of his father. This purpose had become an obsession. So he called for mobilization against what he said was a threatened French invasion.

This was the old familiar call to Englishmen to defend their homes against the aggressor, and the people answered it. Yeoman, serf and villein, armed with scythe and pitchfork and ax, came pouring down to the rendezvous at Portsmouth where the King had assembled the largest fleet in English history.

How the King's Purpose Was Prevented Portsmouth 1205

BELOW HIM AT PORTSMOUTH JOHN COULD SEE THE
harbor crammed with vessels. Never had there been
so large or goodly an assembly of ships. The Cinque
Ports had sent their argosies. These were the five ports
that were called "the gates that open and shut to the
peril or safety of this kingdom." On the downs about
the King was camped the English army. He had sent
the call to arms throughout all England and the
people had answered it. A mighty array had come
prepared with ax and bow to hurl back the invader
with the old Saxon battle cry "Ut! Ut!" or to follow
the King across the Channel and win back the lands
of his father.

The barons were there, too, with William Marshal
and Archbishop Hubert Walter. But John knew that
he could not count on them. He was no longer sure
of any man's loyalty. Some of his barons had deserted
him in Normandy and gone over to Philip, and there
were many here who would serve two masters.

When Marshal and the Archbishop came to him
with grave faces and arguments against war with

Philip, he knew it was as he had feared. "Philip is too strong for us," Marshal said. "He hath taken all your lands across the water."

"When our brave army and our chief men are away, our enemies will come upon us and invade the land," added Hubert Walter.

There were many other arguments and the two councilors spoke long and earnestly. When they could not prevail over the King's will by argument, "They fell down before him and, embracing his knees, restrained him from leaving them, declaring that of a surety if he would not yield to their prayers, they would detain him by force, lest by his departure the whole kingdom be brought to confusion."

The King was now weeping with rage and furiously demanded what *they* proposed to do to save the King's honor and aid his friends beyond the sea.

It was finally decided to send a task force to aid John's friends. The main army was disbanded, and the disappointed hosts returned to their homes muttering that the King had been prevented from destroying his enemies by evil councilors.

To punish the stubborn barons, John now laid a heavy tax upon the whole land, for he was firmly determined that he would yet recover his lost heritage across the Channel.

STEPHEN LANGTON

Of How Langton Was Made Archbishop and How John Forbade Him the Kingdom 1207

JOHN WAS SULLENLY BROODING OVER HIS LOST DOMINions beyond the sea when messengers came with the news of the death of Hubert Walter, Archbishop of Canterbury. "Now for the first time I am King of England," said John as he sighed with relief. Much as he disliked Hubert Walter, who had so often crossed his will, he knew that the Archbishop had

[58]

served England well. He had kept peace and the laws and customs throughout the land in troubled times, although his church complained that he thought too much on temporal affairs.

After the stately funeral, the King told the monks of Canterbury that they would do well to elect as archbishop one whom he would name, for he wanted no watch dog about him such as Hubert had been. Because they feared the King and sought his favor, the monks elected the King's choice, John de Grey, as Archbishop of Canterbury. To show his appreciation, before he left Canterbury the King removed a valuable quantity of Church plate to which he had taken a fancy for his private collection.

The monks had elected the King's candidate with unseemly haste, it soon appeared. Other members of the order had previously chosen a candidate who they now said rightfully claimed the exalted office.

The decision between the two candidates was appealed to Rome. The Pope chose neither. He signified as his choice Cardinal Stephen Langton, who was then dutifully "elected." Langton was an English priest and scholar who had studied many years in Paris. It was he who first divided the Bible text into chapters and verses. This has been a great aid to Bible students ever since. Because of his wisdom and good works, the Pope had made him a cardinal. No better man could have been found for England's primate. But

King John would not agree to this. In his rage and fury he forbade Langton to set foot in England, and he immediately banished the monks of Canterbury.

The Pope, on hearing of John's refusal of his appointment, "was touched to the heart with grief" and sent the Bishop of London to the King with some wholesome advice to yield to God in this matter. But the Pope's instructions did not stop there. If John should continue his rebellious conduct, the Bishop was ordered to lay an interdict on the whole kingdom of England. "If he did not check his boldness by this means, he, the Pope, would lay hands on him still more heavily."

The interdict forbade the clergy to administer the sacraments (although baptism and final absolution were permitted) to all on whom it was laid. The souls of pious Christians quailed at the prospect of this terrible prohibition laid upon the whole land.

John as usual flew into a terrible rage and swore "by God's teeth" that he would send all the prelates of England back to Rome "with their eyes plucked out and their noses slit" if they dared to impose the interdict.

Nevertheless the interdict was pronounced. The great doors of the churches closed; church bells were silenced; the sacraments ceased to be administered. The dead were buried in roads and ditches without prayers or priests. Though the closing of the churches throughout the land might be a holiday for sinners, for the pious it was a terrible calamity.

John in revenge ordered the confiscation of church revenues and property. The King's servants fell greedily upon the clergy and looted the churches and seized the revenues of rich monasteries. When a sheriff brought before the King a robber who had murdered a priest, John said, "He has slain an enemy of mine. Release him and let him go."

John continued to fill his treasury with revenues from the bishops and the looted monasteries, for he said that as the Church no longer performed its duties, its revenues belonged to the crown. He was showing the Pope, the King of France and his own nobles and bishops who was King of England. In his boldness and his pride he laid heavier burdens on the people and increased their griefs beyond measure.

JOHN LACKLAND

THE PROPHECY

The Hands of Rage and Cruelty 1212

As JOHN'S POWER AND WEALTH INCREASED HIS WICK-
edness grew. He inflicted unjust fines on the barons;
some he banished and confiscated their property; and
from those who stayed away from his evil court he
took children and relatives as hostages.

One of his barons named William de Braose fled
to Flanders and died there, but even so John seized
his wife and child and imprisoned them in Windsor
Castle where it was said they died of starvation. He
extracted money from the Jews—sometimes quite
literally, for one of them who refused to hand over
ten thousand marks had a tooth knocked out every
day until on the eighth day he surrendered the ransom money.

John received full credit for these cruelties in the
chronicles written by his enemies, the priests. It may
be a one-sided record and it should be remembered
that such brutalities were the common practice of his
time.

John now turned his energies to subduing the
Welsh and Irish who from the earliest times had been
in a chronic state of revolt. By his effective campaign-
ing he was able, in two years, to defeat these rebels

and establish peace along the borders more effectively than any king before him. When the Welsh again started trouble, he hanged twenty-eight young Welsh-men whom he had been holding as hostages.

Among the strange characters who wandered about the country during these times was a wild and shaggy man called Peter of Wakefield. A professional hermit, Peter went about making people uncomfortable by his prophecies. He said that God had told him that on and after next Ascension Day John would no longer be King of England. This gave gossips a thrill and was repeated all over the land, until everyone was awaiting Ascension Day with great anticipation.

Like many sinful people, the King was a very superstitious man and when this prophecy was brought to him, it made him very uneasy. He had Peter brought before him and respectfully suggested to the holy man that he had made a mistake. But Peter said he was only repeating what God had told him and that he could do nothing about it. John had Peter put in chains, saying that if the prophecy didn't come true Peter would have to take the consequences. Either way, one of them was sure to lose.

Many of the bishops had left England during the interdict, but the Pope ordered his Bishops who remained in the country to pronounce excommunication on the King for his crimes. The bishops, in fear of the King, "were like dumb dogs not daring to bark" and did not publicly announce the excommunication.

Nevertheless, as the sentence of excommunication was published in northern France, it was soon known in England and good Christians of all sorts began absenting themselves from the King's company. This was an opportunity for the resentful baronage and many began secret correspondence with the King of France proposing that he invade England and take over the kingdom.

Stephen Langton and the exiled bishops in France, deciding that this was a fitting time to act against John, went to Rome and informed the Pope "of the diverse rebellions and enormities perpetrated by the King of England from the time of the interdict up to the present time, by unceasing laying the hands of rage and cruelty on the holy Church in opposition to the Lord.

"The Pope then being deeply grieved for the desolation of the kingdom of England, by the advice of his cardinals, bishops and other wise men definitely decreed that John, King of England, be deposed from the throne of that kingdom."

The Pope further ordered the King of France to undertake this business and decreed that he and his successors should hold possession of the kingdom of England forever. He also proclaimed a universal crusade against John and promised that all who proceeded against him would have the protection of the holy Church.

John realized that he was now in a desperate situation and once again issued a call throughout his kingdom to assemble men, arms and munitions against a French invasion. He moved swiftly to meet the threats increasing from every side. But with the Pope and Philip combined in war against him, could he count on the support of his own barons?

Although John had carried on a violent and public quarrel with the Pope, he had nevertheless kept up a confidential negotiation with the Vatican that was always fluid and open to terms.

The papal legate who represented the Pope in his dealings with John was Pandulph, from Milan. Pandulph was an astute man, well aware of the sudden reversals and shifts of ground the King could make when it was to his advantage. Before leaving Rome for England with the Pope's decree against John, he had gone privately to His Holiness to inquire discreetly what should be done if he should find in John unexpected fruits of repentance in these matters. The Pope then dictated a simple form of peace. "If he should agree to it, he might find favor with the Apostolic See," said the Pope as he bade Pandulph farewell.

Sometime later two clerks came from France to the King saying that Pandulph, friend of the Pope, would speak with him on urgent matters. John did not know what the next move would be but he sensed that something was in the wind and that he might turn it to his advantage.

The Great Assembly at Barham Down 1213

ALL ENGLAND WAS AWAITING THE INVASION. IT WAS
known that the fleet of Philip of France was gathered
at Calais to transport the French King's mighty army
to the shores of England. Behind the King of France
was a more powerful foe, John's arch enemy the Pope.
Pope Innocent III had commanded the French King
to invade England and depose John from his throne
forever. The barons of England were now absolved
from all allegiance to the excommunicated King. All
this, John believed, was the work of Stephen Langton.

John acted quickly. To the bailiffs of all ports
went the warrant ordering all ships to be listed,
manned, provisioned and assembled at Portsmouth on
the Sunday after Ash Wednesday.

To all the sheriffs of the kingdom went the following letter:

"John, King of England, gives warning by good
agents to the earls, barons, knights and all free and
serving men, whoever they be, or by whatever tenure
they hold, who ought to have or may procure arms,
who have made homage and sworn allegiance to us,
that, as they regard us as well as themselves and all

their own property, they be at Dover at the end of the coming Lent, equipped with horses and arms and with all they can provide, to defend our person and their persons, and the land of England."

They came swarming down by thousands to answer the King's call—to defend the land of England once again as they had done so often before. There were men of all ages and conditions—a rabble of rustics, untrained, armed with axes, pitchforks and scythes and ready to fight with their bare hands if need be for England. In a short time the provisions of this rabble-in-arms became exhausted. Then the regular army took charge, established discipline, sent back the untrained volunteers, and organized the freemen, the archers, crossbow men, and men-at-arms. The earls and barons came riding in with their knights and cavalry and trained fighting men. Shortly an organized army of sixty thousand fighting men, trained and well armed, was camped on Barham Down to hold England against the foe.

The King counted on his fleet for the first line of defense. Through the castle window he could see the great armada that crowded the harbor. He hoped to drown Philip and all his men before a Frenchman could set foot on English soil.

Of How King John Surrendered His Kingdom
1213

PANDULPH, THE POPE'S LEGATE, WAS A DISCREET AND subtle man possessed of great dignity. His long face was dark and his large eyes had a kindly glow under their heavy lids. He sat facing the King across the oaken table. Out of earshot on each side stood groups of whispering dignitaries in their official robes.

The King began the interview suavely with an account of the immense army that had responded to his call. He could depend on every man, he said, and his fleet was far greater than that of the French. Indeed, from the castle walls much of this force could actually be seen in impressive array. John boastfully said there was not a prince under heaven against whom his army could not defend England.

Pandulph listened respectfully until the King had finished and then spoke. He admired the strength and powers of the English King, he said, but he had just come from France where Philip had assembled an equally splendid fleet and an army of horses and men, together with the clergy whom he intended to

[69]

restore to their *stolen* lands in England (with a significant glance at the King). No doubt King John would prevail, except—and here Pandulph leaned forward on the table, touching the tips of his long fingers slowly together and gazing absently toward the window—"Except that the King of France holds papers of fealty and subjection from almost all the nobles of England. On which account," he added, "he feels secure of bringing the business he has undertaken to a most successful termination." Here Pandulph paused, leaning back in his chair. "I have seen these papers," he resumed. "We of the Church have opportunities to learn many things not commonly known, for knowledge of the world's doings comes to us from all quarters in many ways."

John's eyes narrowed and glowed green. He had suspected as much of his barons all along. It was what he would have done if he were one of them. The muscles of his jaws swelled as he ground his teeth in fury, but he said not a word. He was thinking fast for the ground was slipping from under him. The prophecy of Peter of Wakefield flashed through his mind and he swallowed uneasily.

"However," went on Pandulph hopefully, "in case you should repent and atone these would be the terms for your absolution and return to the Holy Church." He handed John the paper containing the papal terms.

John leaned forward, reading the cramped script half aloud. "We solemnly and absolutely swear to abide by the commands of our lord the Pope, that we will observe strict peace and afford full security to those venerable men, Stephen, Archbishop of Canterbury——" (with a long list of his most hated bishops) "——make full restitution of the confiscated property, protect their restored rights, etc., to assign and grant to God and His Holy Apostles Peter and Paul, and the holy Church of Rome, our Mother, and to our lord Pope Innocent and his Catholic successors, the whole kingdom of England and the whole kingdom of Ireland . . . and henceforth we retain and hold these countries from him and the Church of Rome as vice regent and this we declare in the presence of this learned man, Pandulph——"

Here Pandulph pointed out that, if John agreed to these terms, he would become the champion and defender of England for God and the Pope; that the French King would not dare attack and that his enemies, the rebellious barons, could be excommunicated and subject to fine and forfeit of their entire possessions if they continued to oppose him.

As Pandulph talked a sudden illumination brightened the prospects in John's mind. Here was truly a wonderful solution to his desperate situation. If he took this step it would completely turn the tables on all his enemies. Through all Christendom he would be proclaimed as a defender of the Church. If attacked he would be called a martyr. Suddenly a wonderful sense of his own piety came over him. This agreement was a beautiful combination of holiness with expediency. He would do it.

On the eve of Ascension Day, May 15, 1213, he met Pandulph and the nobles of England at the house of the Knights Templars near Dover. There the King assigned and granted to the Pope the entire kingdoms of England and Ireland.

The agreements were delivered in writing to Pandulph to be taken to Pope Innocent. John gave his solemn oath ending, "I will assist in holding and defending the heritage of St. Peter, and particularly the kingdoms of England and Ireland against all men, to the utmost of my power. So may God and the Holy Gospel help me, Amen."

One dark cloud still hung over him. The next day was the dreaded Ascension Day when Peter of Wakefield had prophesied John would no longer be king. All England hung on the prophecy, but the day passed pleasantly. The King feasted with his friends in a pavilion especially set up for the occasion. But to make it all the more memorable, he ordered the hermit to be tied to a horse's tail and dragged through the streets of the town, after which he was to be hanged on a gibbet, together with his son. To many this seemed a pity for the facts proved that the prophet did not tell a falsehood. John, having given his realm to the Pope, was legally no longer its King.

Of How the King of France Was Greatly Discomfited

1213

HAVING ACCOMPLISHED HIS MISSION, PANDULPH HAD gone at once to France with eight thousand pounds for the exiled English clergy and the news that more indemnities for their wrongs awaited them in England. His interview with the French King was a painful surprise to that monarch. Pandulph made it clear that the invasion must be called off, for Philip would now be attacking the Pope. The King was furious. He had spent sixty thousand pounds in preparation, he said. Besides, he had undertaken the invasion at the command of the Pope and for the remission of his sins, which were considerable. To sum up, he would go on with the invasion, Pope or no Pope.

But now Philip's ally, the Count of Flanders, refused to go along with him. The Count had himself made a private treaty with the King of England. He maintained Philip had robbed him and besides, he added piously, "The war is unjust." Whereupon, the French invasion fleet being still at hand, Philip ordered it to set sail without delay and attack Flanders. The Count of Flanders immediately sent an urgent demand to John for help.

As the English fleet was not now needed for defense, John sent it immediately to Flanders under command of the Earl of Salisbury. Shortly thereafter a great fleet of five hundred ships carrying seven hundred knights and many foot soldiers arrived at the port of Swine.

To the surprise of the English, they found this harbor crowded with a great armada of the French King's ships. There appeared to be scarcely anyone on guard, for the French forces were out looting the Flemish towns and countryside. The English at once pounced upon the enemy's ships and captured and looted the whole fleet. They found the ships loaded to the gunnels with corn, wine, flour, meat, arms, and all the munitions of war. Every English soldier and sailor was soon loaded with plunder such as had not come to England since "Arthur went to conquer it."

Three hundred of the ships with their cargoes were sent to England and a hundred looted and burned. This was the English navy's first great victory, though it was more a gift of Providence than a planned engagement. The Earl of Salisbury went ashore and attacked the French on land, but Philip and his army had arrived by this time and the English were beaten back. The French King was so disgusted at the destruction of his fleet that he ordered his remaining ships to be set on fire and his army to return to France.

This sudden turn of affairs put King John in the very best of humor. It was a splendid beginning for his plans and he sent a large sum of money to the Count of Flanders with the object of encouraging him to bedevil the French King as much as possible.

Of How the King Greatly Humbled Himself 1213

WITH A GREAT ARMY NOW ASSEMBLED, JOHN PREPARED to invade France. But his northern barons whom he called on to support him in this venture refused to follow him. On this occasion they said piously that they could not possibly consider it until he was publicly absolved from his excommunication.

John thereupon invited his old enemy, Stephen Langton, and twenty-four of the banished churchmen, to return from France and receive indemnity for the property they had been deprived of and all their other rights.

Now that John was the Pope's vassal and he must make peace with the Archbishop Stephen and be publicly absolved by him, he planned to dramatize his repentance. Langton and his bishops landed at Dover and proceeded to meet the King at Winchester. John, like all the Angevins, was a good actor, though he had not the style and figure of his heroic brother Richard. He was quite aware that the role of a repentant sinner was the most sentimental one in the Christian world and he was looking forward to playing this part with genuine drama and emotion.

As the bishops approached Winchester, John went forth to meet them clad in his royal attire. His eyes

streaming tears, he prostrated himself at the feet of his ancient enemy Stephen and bowed his head to the ground. The bishops were not prepared for this excess of repentance and respectfully tried to raise him from the ground. He was a heavy man but they finally got him to his feet. With a bishop supporting each arm, he was led sobbing bitterly to the great doors of the cathedral.

Even the nobles were weeping by this time, and the King's groanings and gaspings were dreadful to hear. From within, the voices of the choir burst forth with the words of the majestic Fiftieth Psalm:

The mighty God, even the Lord, hath spoken, and called the earth from the rising of the sun unto the going down thereof. Out of Zion, the perfection of beauty God hath shined.

On the steps of the altar the Archbishop formally absolved John according to the solemn ritual of the Church.

As the King gained control of his voice he brokenly swore on the holy gospels that he would love the Holy Church and its ordained members; he would renew all the good laws of his ancestors, especially those of King Edward, and would annul all the bad ones; and he would judge all his subjects according to the laws of his courts. Seeing that this was having a fine effect, he went on promising everyone all the rights he could think of.

Everyone had expected a good show, but the King had broken all records. There had been nothing to equal it since his father, Henry the Second, had bared his back at the tomb of St. Thomas à Becket and insisted on being whipped by the priests.

After it was all over, the most important people were invited to feast with the King. They all sat together at the King's table and talked and laughed, and made merry together like good politicians who knew that in a short time they would all be fighting one another again like cats and dogs.

Next day the King sent letters to all the sheriffs of the kingdom ordering them to send four liege men from each town in their demesne to St. Albans on the fourth of August, that he might inquire into the losses and confiscated property of each bishop and how much was due to each. Later, historians said that this was probably the first step toward those gatherings of the representatives of the people that would some day become the English Parliament.

HENRY II

How Stephen Langton Found King Henry's Charter 1213

STEPHEN LANGTON HAD RETURNED TO ENGLAND AFTER many years, studious years spent in Paris and busy years in Rome where, for his usefulness and holiness, he had been made a cardinal. For the last six years he had been the exiled Archbishop of Canterbury waiting in France until peace should be made between the Pope and King John.

Now he was a power in England, for the King was the Pope's vassal and must heed the Archbishop's council. Because he was a brave and humble man,

[81]

Stephen had returned determined to serve the people of his troubled country with what wisdom and strength God had given him.

He had not long to wait. When the King had summoned his northern barons to follow him to the wars in France, they had refused and returned to their castles in the north. Furiously, the King collected his army of mercenaries and marched toward Nottingham, swearing he would have vengeance on these traitorous dogs. So the King was in one of his most dangerous moods when the Archbishop came to him and firmly demanded that he should not begin a civil war, but that he should have the barons brought to trial according to the ancient customs of England which he had sworn at his absolution to obey.

More enraged than ever, John shouted at Langton to mind his own business, which was the Church, and ordered the royal army to march after the barons. But the Archbishop boldly replied that he had the power to interdict all who disobeyed the Church. At this threat, John sullenly yielded. It was Stephen's first clash with the King and he had won.

None knew better than the Archbishop that neither the word of the King nor the nobles could be trusted. Law and justice must rest on firmer ground. England had in time past been ruled by noble kings. Had they left some solemn charter to steady the kingdom in times to come?

Langton searched long and patiently among the

dusty parchments of the ancient records. At last he came upon what he sought. It was a charter granted and sealed by John's great-grandfather, Henry the First, at his coronation. This was a time when newly made kings were apt to be generous, and Henry I had it written in this charter that he would defend the Church and keep the good laws of the land and abolish bad ones. The terms were somewhat vague and the very existence of the charter had long ago been forgotten, but the Archbishop felt it would serve now for a beginning. It was an answer to his prayer. He could strengthen and expand this document into a charter that was strong and clear enough to bind kings and establish rights and justice in England for all men forever.

The Archbishop knew that the nobles cared little for the rights of lesser men, but they were the only power in England that could restrain the King. For many years, the nobles had endured John's insults until now their hidden enmity was smoldering beneath the surface ready to burst into rebellion. Now the time had come to enlist their power to force a charter from the King.

Langton called an assemblage of the churchmen of England to St. Paul's in London and purposely included many noble earls and barons for the good of their souls, as he put it. Many of the most powerful of them attended. After the solemnities and church matters were concluded, the Archbishop called the barons aside for a very private conference. When all the doors were closed, he said, "Did you hear, my lords, how, when I absolved the King on that day at Winchester, I made him swear that he would do away with unjust laws and would recall good laws, and cause them to be observed by all in the kingdom?" He paused as the barons nodded gravely.

"It will concern you to know," the Archbishop went on, "that a charter of Henry the First has been found by which you may, if you wish it, recall your long lost rights and your former condition."

There was a stir among the crowd for such words had not been heard in England for many a year. "Read, my lord bishop, read," eager voices called out.

Langton signaled to a priest who came forward with the ancient charter and read it. As the import of the Archbishop's intent began to dawn upon the nobles, there was a clamorous discussion. "We will stand for our rights," said some. "And die for them too, if need be," added others. When they asked Langton if he would aid their cause, he faithfully promised to do so as far as lay in his power. So they swore a solemn oath upon the altar to maintain this cause and stand together when the moment for action came. Until then they would separate, keeping secret all that had transpired.

John had been sending large sums of the taxpayers' money to his allies in Flanders to enable them to harass King Philip. They were to ravage Philip's territories and destroy his castles. This they were doing with fire and sword, until the blackened and ravaged countryside lay a barren wasteland of famine and death.

John was greatly cheered by this good news. Now, he thought, was the time for his long planned attack upon the King of France. He himself would lead, and when he had won the fight and regained his lost provinces he would be strong enough to subdue his implacable enemies, the barons of England. "He hated, like a viper's poison, all the men of noble rank in the kingdom, and especially Sayer de Quency, Robert Fitz-Walter, and Stephen, Archbishop of Canterbury. He sent a large sum of money to the Pope on condition that he would, when opportunity occurred, endeavor to abase the Archbishop of Canterbury and excommunicate the barons of England, and he eagerly longed for this, that he might glut his evil disposition by disinheriting, imprisoning and slaying them when excommunicated. And these plans, which he most wickedly raked up, he more wickedly carried into execution, as will be related hereafter."*

With these thoughts in his mind, John departed with a large army for France and began the endless game of castle-taking with Philip in the province of Poitou.

* *Flowers of History,* by Roger of Wendover.

[85]

Of How Philip Smote His Enemies and King John's Return to England

THE KING OF FRANCE WAS SORELY PRESSED BY HIS enemies from both the north and south. For John had crossed to Poitou with an army of mercenaries and was ravaging the southern countryside with fire and sword. Along Philip's northern borders the Count of Flanders, the German Emperor Otto (John's nephew) and the Earl of Salisbury were causing great devastation.

The castle of La Roche-au-Moine, which John was besieging, was about to surrender when he learned that the French King's son, Louis, was advancing upon him to raise the siege. John was eager for battle, for he had the stronger force. Then the disaster that ever pursued him struck him. The nobles of Poitou, on learning of Louis' approach, deserted the English King, saying they would not risk a pitched battle with the French in the open. His forces thus weakened, John retreated, though he was still sure that his allies on the north would destroy Philip.

Attacked on both sides, the French King urgently summoned barons and knights, townsmen and yeomen—everyone who would fight for France in her hour of peril. Right loyally they came in eager hordes to their King's call.

The French force met the combined English, German and Flemish host at the bridge of Bouvines, where Philip drew up his line of defense with its back to the river. The July sun glinted on the spears, helmets and bright banners. Trumpets sounded and the great war horses tossed their heads.

As usual, about the only plans of battle on either side were simply the equivalent of "Up and at 'em!" The Flemings advanced with a mighty rush of foot soldiers, forcing back the French King. He was thrown to the ground but, leaping up, mounted a fresh horse and rushed again into the battle, leading the French knighthood who lowered their spears and charged in a great wave of iron, plowing deep into the Flemish rabble of footmen. These now gave way, and the French knights pushed forward and surrounded the Emperor Otto, who held the enemy center. The Emperor laid about him with his great sword, holding off all his attackers. But with his troops fleeing everywhere, Otto soon found himself fighting almost alone and, mounting a fresh horse, fled, barely escaping capture. The counts of Flanders and Holland, who had boasted proudly of their valor, now made for the rear at top speed.

Choking clouds of dust filled the burning air. In the wild melee, it was difficult to tell friend from foe. The battle had become a chaos of thrusting, slashing swords and spears in hand-to-hand encounter.

The fighting Bishop of Beauvais, whose motto was "When you see a head, hit it," now charged the English might, swinging his great iron mace. His target was the Earl of Salisbury, who had been so successful in destroying Philip's fleet a short time before, and who was now holding off the massed attack of the whole knighthood of France. With his iron club, the Bishop gave the Earl a terrific thump on the head which knocked him to the ground. Before he could rise he was taken prisoner and held for ransom.

The English now began to flee and the pursuing French were eagerly capturing as many of the nobles as they could for their ransom value.

It was a glorious victory for France. For a week citizens and students danced and feasted and celebrated in the streets of Paris.

When news reached John of Philip's victory at Bouvines he was greatly dismayed and disheartened, for since he had become reconciled to the Church he had believed that the angels would fight on his side. In fact he had counted on them. And now, like his nobles, they had shown they could not be trusted!

"Since I became reconciled to God, and submitted myself and my kingdoms to the Church of Rome, woe is me. Nothing has gone prosperously with me, and everything unlucky has happened to me," muttered John bitterly. Could it be that piety did not pay? he wondered.

RUNNYMEDE

Of How King John Denied His Barons 1215

John returned to England after the battle of Bouvines in a very bad Angevin temper. It was not improved by what he found awaiting him at home. The barons had ceased fighting among themselves and were united against him and on the verge of rebellion. What was this rumor about a charter? John wondered. No doubt someone had been putting ideas into their thick heads. This must be the work of his old enemy Stephen Langton, he was sure.

The King found himself almost alone, for there were scarcely a dozen knights on whom he could rely. There was no one he could trust. He swore he would never submit to the barons and sign their charter. But there was no use rolling on the floor and chewing wood. He must settle with the barons face to face. He summoned them to meet him after Christmas and to bring their demands to him at London in the New Temple.

When John entered the crowded hall of the New Temple in London, the barons all stood as he seated himself on the dais. He recognized the look of sullen hate in every face. The nobles were all dressed in full mail. The King well knew what this meant.

At a sign from John, the barons' spokesman stood forth, saying that the King had sworn at his absolution at Winchester to restore the ancient laws and liberties of King Edward, and they would have him renew them with his oath and seal *now*.

John checked his fury, for he saw that he was helpless and in great danger. He must parley for time.

"Your demands are a matter of importance and difficulty," he replied calmly. "I ask you for a truce until the end of Easter, that I may with due deliberation satisfy you as well as the dignity of my crown. Let the Archbishop of Canterbury, Bishop Ely, and William Marshal be my sureties that I will satisfy you all."

It was fair spoken and the meeting adjourned until Easter.

John had succeeded in his maneuver. Now, he thought, he must take whatever safeguards he could against these traitors, as he termed the barons. He at once assumed the Cross, which meant that he became a Crusader and thus gained the Church's protection. Moreover, he caused all the nobles of England to renew their oath of allegiance to him against all men. Still he did not feel safe.

In the meantime, Langton and his clerks and William Marshal were very busy, for they were rewriting and strengthening the vague terms of the old charter. The revised charter must state precisely the rights of the nobles and the Church. There must be some security and some right and justice for the common people of England as well; not for just the few, but for all men. And to this end Langton was consulting with the wise men of England, though in truth these were but few.

Easter came and the nobles began to gather at Stamford in open rebellion against the King. The call to join the revolt had been sent to the barons and knights throughout all England. Dressed in mail, a mighty gathering of England's chivalry came riding in with banners and lances—two thousand knights with squires and foot soldiers and men-at-arms.

Realizing his danger, John sent Langton and Marshal to meet with the barons at Brackley on April 27 and to find out exactly what were the rights they demanded. The archbishop returned with a draft of their demands, many of which the primate himself had written. He also delivered a statement from the barons to the effect that unless they received satisfaction from the King in the matter of the charter, they would immediately take possession of his castles.

As he addressed the King, Langton's manner was respectful and even sympathetic but his tone was firm and unyielding for he knew that the full might of the barons of England was behind him. And although the King considered him his worst enemy he well knew that the Archbishop stood like a rock for justice before God and the law.

John listened sullenly as the articles of the charter were read one by one, for he had no power to do otherwise.

The first demand stated that the Church should have her liberties and the rights of free elections. The King nodded, for this was an old quarrel which he had already settled with the Pope.

Next, heirs and widows were to have their inheritances and their rights to these respected. It was said that the King had made himself everyone's heir by appropriating his subjects' estates for himself. Debts must be properly collected instead of the King's taking everything the debtor owned, as had often been his custom.

At this point in the reading of the articles John muttered gloomily, "What is the world coming to?"

The Archbishop read on:

Towns and cities were to have their liberties and free customs. (This meant the loss of another source of royal blackmail.)

The King must summon the great council of the realm to meet at specified times and places and for stated purposes and to lay assessments and taxes. (This meant that the barons would have power to regulate the King's expenses.)

John started to rise from his chair but sank back with a groan. Gritting his teeth, he said, "Read on."

The Archbishop smiled sympathetically and went on:

When penalties were imposed for offenses, the freeman, the merchant and the villein must be allowed to retain their tools, goods and means of sustenance. (This was the first time the villein or common man was mentioned in the charter.)

"NO FREEMAN SHALL BE TAKEN OR IMPRISONED, OR DISSEIZED, OR OUTLAWED, OR BANISHED, OR ANYWAYS DESTROYED, NOR WILL WE PASS UPON HIM, NOR WILL WE SEND UPON HIM, UNLESS BY THE LAWFUL JUDGMENT OF HIS PEERS, OR BY THE LAW OF THE LAND. WE WILL SELL TO NO MAN, WE WILL NOT DENY TO ANY MAN, EITHER JUSTICE OR RIGHT."

Here Langton paused and looked sharply at the King.

John swore horribly. "You have taken off my right arm!" he screamed. "You have made the King of England no better than a slave subject to the meanest villein in the land."

"I fear, Sire, that thus it must be," said the Archbishop gravely, "that justice and liberty under God may prevail for all in England."

"Ere you are done the King of England will be the jest of all Christendom. Go on with this foul mockery," and John gestured feebly.

Langton read on:

"We will immediately give up all hostages and charters delivered unto us by our English subjects as securities for their keeping the peace and yielding us faithful service.

"If anyone has been dispossessed or deprived by us, without lawful judgment of his peers, of his lands, castles, liberties, or right, we will forthwith restore them to him, and if any dispute arises upon this head, let the matter be decided by the five and twenty barons hereafter mentioned, for the preservation of the peace."

Another article stated that all foreign troops should be sent out of the kingdom.

John passed his hand over his face, for he was too shaken to speak. Beads of sweat broke out on his forehead.

"No man shall be taken or imprisoned on the accusation of a woman for the death of any other than her husband."

"Perhaps there is some small comfort for a man in this," muttered the King.

Langton read on:

"All unjust and illegal fines made by us, and all amerciements imposed unjustly and contrary to the law of the land, shall be entirely given up, or else be left to the decision of the five and twenty barons hereafter mentioned for the preservation of the peace."

"What meaneth this babbling of five and twenty barons?" interrupted the King.

"It pertaineth to the enforcement of the charter, Sire, that some security of its performance may be secured, for it is further writ here, my lord, that 'we do give and grant our subjects the underwritten security, namely that the barons may choose five and twenty barons of the kingdom whom they think convenient who shall take care, with all their might, to hold and observe and cause to be observed, the peace and liberties we have granted them, and by this our present charter confirmed in this manner.' "

The Archbishop paused, for the King's face was terrible to behold. After a pause Stephen Langton continued to read:

"That is to say that if we, our justiciars, our bailiffs, or our officers shall in any circumstance have failed in the performance of them toward any person, or shall have broken through any of these articles of peace and security, the said five and twenty barons, together with the community of the whole kingdom, shall distrain and distress us in all the ways in which they shall be able, by seizing our castles, lands, possessions, and in any other manner they can, till the grievance is redressed according to their pleasure."

"By God's teeth," shouted the King, "you have by this given me five and twenty overlords and hath instructed them to treason and rebellion in overthrowing the kingdom at their will. Why, among these unjust demands, did not the barons ask for my kingdom also?" he added bitterly. "Tell them that I will never grant them! These vain visions are without reason. These visionary liberties would make me a slave to this pack of traitors! Go tell them this is my final answer."

Marshal and the Archbishop argued and reasoned but this only aggravated the King's fury; and so they returned to the barons with the story of their interview.

The barons immediately appointed Robert Fitz-Walter as their commander in chief and designated him "Marshal of the army of God and the holy Church."

The army moved on Northampton and laid siege to the castle. This was a declaration of war.

John saw that he had now to deal with armed rebellion, and it was no comfort that even the few nobles who still seemed loyal were daily deserting till there were not enough left to hold his castles. He sent messengers to the Pope telling of his dire peril and calling for swift aid. In France his agents were raising an army of foreign mercenaries. But it would take time for help to reach him from abroad, and meanwhile his enemies were busy.

The barons' first attack was not successful, for the King's castle of Northampton held out and after fifteen days the siege was abandoned. But secret couriers soon brought encouraging news. The barons might now take London if their army came at once, for certain rich citizens were their friends and would aid them.

By a swift night march the barons' army reached London at daybreak. The gates were open, and the streets deserted. The citizens were at church, for it was Sunday. The barons took the capital without striking a blow.

How John Deceitfully Gave Consent to the Charter

June 15 1215

WHEN THE KING LEARNED THAT HE HAD LOST LONDON, his indignation as well as his fears were mightily increased, for he saw that he was deserted now by all. The barons on their side greatly rejoiced, and sent letters to those earls and barons and knights who appeared still to hold to the King, advising them with threats to the safety of their persons and property to abandon a king who was perjured and who warred against his barons.

John knew that now he could no longer defend his castles, as only a handful of knights were still loyal to him. But he had been in desperate situations before, and he swore he would yet outwit these stupid nobles. He sent William Marshal to the barons with a message saying that for the sake of peace and for the exaltation and honor of his kingdom, he would willingly grant them the laws and liberties they required. Marshal negotiated an arrangement with the barons whereby they would meet the King at the field of Runnymede, between Windsor and Staines on the Thames, on the 15th of June, 1215.

There was great rejoicing in the camp of the barons, for they deemed they had at last broken the King's will. Some, especially among the younger ones, did not remember that John was most dangerous when he seemed most willing to make promises.

Stephen Langton had enlarged the articles of the Barons into a charter of sixty-four articles prepared for the King's seal. Well he knew that neither the King nor the barons were respectors of promises, and that between the wickedness of them all the devil himself could not choose. However, he was convinced that once the King's seal was affixed, the charter would remain in effect long after this King and his nobles had gone. That night ere he slept, as was his custom he opened the Bible that had been ever his guide and read from the Book of the prophet Isaiah:

"The Spirit of the Lord God is upon me; because the Lord hath anointed me to preach good tidings unto the meek; He hath sent me to bind up the broken-hearted, to proclaim liberty to the captives, and the opening of the prison to them that are bound; to comfort all that mourn."

RUNNYMEDE

Runnymede, June 15 1215

ENGLAND IN JUNE WAS A FAIR GARDEN, AND THROUGH its flower-strewn meadows the Thames wound down to London town, reflecting white cloud drifts and blue sky in its shining surface.

At Runnymede brave banners and fluttering penons filled the air with dancing color, the pavilions of earl and baron were splendid in silk and cloth of gold, and the heraldic emblems of the nobility blazed in the bright sunshine. For the great lords of England were come with all their strength to humble their craven King. Squires in bright liveries attended the great war horses, their polished flanks gleaming in the sun. The barons wore their chain mail hauberks and belted swords, for this was a display of armed power arrayed for action. Grim lords bore themselves proudly, for never had the nobles of England so restrained their King. Behind knightly pageant, a ragged army of soldiers and men-at-arms lounged and diced, idly wondering what and when would be the next campaign of their proud lords and masters.

Suddenly a blare of trumpets announced that the King had arrived at his pavilion. There were no traces on his calm features of the insane rages of previous days, for John was a superb actor and on this occasion he needed to muster all the dignity at his command to show a semblance of royal authority.

Stephen Langton in his Archbishop's mitre and stole embroidered in gold, and William Marshal in hauberk of chain mail, representing the King, met the rebel barons and read the charter aloud. Langton then brought it to the King. The great moment had come. The King rose, paused and, with a malicious jab, affixed the royal seal to the charter.

The barons then pledged anew their homage to the King.

After weeks of discussion and negotiation, the final ceremony was completed in one day. Again the trumpets sounded. The King mounted his horse and led his little retinue back to Windsor Castle.

Immediately clerks made copies of the great charter —Magna Charta, as it was called—and these were sent to the King's sheriffs to be read in every shire in England. The charter with the King's seal was now the written law of the land.

Although the wording of the charter sounded as though John had freely granted it to his people, he had been forced into signing it by his barons and the will of the people. More than to any other person, this was due to the efforts of Stephen Langton, who, since his arrival in England, had toiled patiently to find lawful means to control the unchecked power and personal will of a wicked King.

The clearly defined rights stated in the charter now stood above the will of the King. Many of the unwritten ancient customs were defined in the articles of the charter. Tenants, farmers, townsmen, merchants, villeins and freemen as well as the barons and the Church were assured their traditional rights.

The provision that "no scutage or aid shall be imposed in our realm save by the common council of the realm" was a first step toward parliamentary government.

The love of right and justice of the old Anglo-Saxon freemen lived again in the spirit of the Magna Charta. It was a signpost pointing the way on the long road to new and greater freedoms and to the beginnings of liberty, equality, fraternity and democracy in later centuries.

John, obedient to the terms of the charter, sent back all foreign soldiers and promised to restore all estates wrongfully withheld from his barons.

At this moment it seemed that the danger of civil war had been averted. As a means of enforcing the charter "five and twenty barons" were appointed to watch over the King and to see that the provisions of the charter were observed.

How King John Hid Himself and Laid Plots Against the Barons

IT HAD BEEN A BITTER DAY FOR JOHN, BUT HE HAD acted his part in the ceremony with kingly perfection. As he rode back with his little band of knights toward Windsor Castle again the fire of his anger burned hot within him and he swore he would punish the traitorous dogs who called themselves his nobles.

That night, as he tossed on his bed, he plotted elaborate schemes of vengeance. He of course would not keep a word of the charter he had signed, except (and here he ground his teeth) for the twenty-five barons assigned to watch him in order to see that the laws of the charter were kept. "They have given me five and twenty over kings!" he screamed in torment. But as his rage passed, his mind cleared and subtly he planned the undoing of his enemies.

He rode south to the seacoast and took refuge in Dover Castle. Here he was safe from attack while he waited and planned. As he looked seaward to France

and Rome, his hopes rose. He would smite his enemies with two swords. First the sword of Spirit, for
the Pope was his liege lord, and John had called on
him for help; secondly, there was the sword of armies
temporal. For this he sent word to the governors of
all his castles to arm and provision themselves against
instant attack. His agents across the channel in the
French provinces were hiring all who would come to
England for high pay and loot to meet at Dover come
Michaelmas.

The Siege of Rochester 1215

IN LONDON THE BARONS FEASTED AND DRANK WINE, rejoicing that the King had fled. There were rumors that he had left the kingdom and would never return. Others said he was hiding on the coast among the fishermen and that he had become a pirate.

The younger barons in their folly said they would now have Louis, the King of France's son, rule over them. To celebrate their recent victory tournaments and joustings were held in the fields near London and a lady gave away a bear as a prize.

The older barons who knew John better withdrew to their castles in the north and fortified them against war, for they knew that the King was most dangerous when he seemed badly beaten. They had not long to wait. A letter arrived from the Pope advising the nobles of England "to make reparation to the King and his followers for the harm and injuries you have inflicted upon him. If you act otherwise you may be reduced to such straits from which you will not be able to escape without much trouble." This threat only made the barons more determined to harass the King with all their might. Then news came that a host of foreign mercenaries in the service of the King had landed at Dover and that John was advancing on London with a great army.

The castle of Rochester was one of the strongest fortresses in England and whoever held it was master of the approach to London. The King had entrusted it to Archbishop Stephen, but he had delivered it over to the barons. And the barons meant to keep it. So now they called on William d'Albiney, a man bold and tried in war, and sent him with a strong force to hold the castle against the King's advance.

William and his one hundred and twenty-four knights had barely time to occupy the castle and take what provisions the town afforded when the swarming hosts of John's army surrounded the castle and assaulted it day and night with ceaseless fury. Great stone-throwing engines hurled huge rocks against the walls until a breach was made. Through this the attackers swarmed in wild rushes but they were thrown back. Meanwhile the defenders on the walls flung down boiling pitch, molten lead and stones upon the men-at-arms who attempted to scale the walls with ladders.

While all this was going on the barons had sallied forth from London to relieve the siege as they had sworn to William d'Albiney they would do if he were besieged. But when their scouts returned with reports of the size and power of the King's forces the barons came to a sudden halt.

"Although only a mild south wind was blowing in their faces which does not generally annoy anyone," the whole company of not-so-valorous lords and knights turned around and rode hastily back to London. There they resumed their knightly exploits of throwing dice, feasting and high times.

The siege of Rochester raged on with unabated fury for three months. The ceaseless assaults of the King's forces were thrown back with fearful losses by the desperate defenders, for they knew that if the castle fell they would receive no mercy from the King. But provisions in the castle had dwindled until the famished knights were forced to eat their precious horses as a last resort.

By this time most of the outer wall had been demolished and the King's soldiers had driven the defenders into the castle keep. Now sappers began to tunnel under its walls, setting up wooden props to support the stonework above. They filled this tunnel with faggots and carcasses of forty fat hogs and set fire to it. The tower collapsed in the roaring flames, but William d'Albiney and his knights still held out in the part of the donjon that was still intact.

Not until long after the last scrap of food had been devoured did the gaunt and battered defenders surrender.

The King had suffered heavy losses in the siege and he revengefully ordered every prisoner to be hanged on a gallows in front of the army.

Savarie de Mauleton was one of the King's nobles

who had a high respect for courage, and when enemies such as these showed it he honored them for it. Now he came to the King and pleaded for the lives of the doomed prisoners who stood in chains before the gallows.

"If you now order us to hang these men," he warned, "the barons, our enemies, will perhaps by a like event take me or other nobles of your army and, following your example, hang us; therefore do not let this happen, for in such case no one will fight in your cause."

John knew well enough the grim logic of this argument and its effect on his soldiers. Reluctantly he reprieved the condemned garrison. The knights were thrown in prison, the rest held for ransom, and only a few of the crossbow men who had caused the most terrible damage to his men were hanged.

This victory represented a turning of the tide in John's fortunes. As he advanced northward, castle after castle surrendered. John gathered the plunder to pay his savage mercenaries, who looted and burned without mercy as they advanced until all the eastern half of England to the Scottish border had fallen to the King.

In London the rebel barons continued their high living and low thinking. They had contrived a wonderful scheme whereby they would destroy John without having to do any fighting at all themselves. To carry out their scheme, they sent word to the King of France proposing that his son Louis should invade England with a large army. If he did this, they promised they would place Louis on the throne. Philip thought this an excellent idea. But it was not so simple as it sounded, for the Pope was John's friend and would surely oppose any such action.

Of How the Pope Rebuked the King's Enemies 1215

JOHN'S ENVOYS HAD REPORTED TO THE POPE THE MAT-
ter of the Magna Charta and the action of the barons,
complaining that "they flew to arms, mounted their
horses, and demanded from the King that the aforesaid laws and liberties should be confirmed to them,
and the King, through fear of an attack from them,
did not dare to refuse what they required." When the
charter was read to the Pope he was very annoyed and
said, "Are the barons of England endeavoring to
drive John from the throne of his kingdom?"

He promptly condemned and forever annulled the
said charter of grants of the liberties of the kingdom
of England. To make this still clearer he added that
he entirely condemned an agreement of this kind
and "forbid the said King, under penalty of excommunication, to keep, and the barons and their accom-
plices to compel him to keep, either the charter or
the bonds or securities which have been given for its
observance, and he altogether quashed the same so
that they may never have any validity."

Furthermore he excommunicated the barons of
England for their rebelliousness in not desisting from
their persecution of the King. In acting as he did the

[114]

Pope was being quite logical, for England was now legally his dominion and John his vassal. In turn, the barons were certainly the King's vassals and on that account owed him obedience. They had not only been disobedient but had set up their own rules and forced the King to agree to them. In all this the Pope had not been consulted, though he certainly should have been. Under these conditions the only possible thing he could do was to "altogether annul and quash" the Magna Charta.

John also accused Stephen Langton of conniving with the barons and giving them favor and advice in their attempt to expel him from the throne of the kingdom. The Pope instructed Langton to announce the excommunication of the barons in all the churches of England. But the Archbishop had neglected to do this and as a result the bishops had suspended him from entering the church and performing divine service.

Langton made the long journey to Rome to ask absolution from the sentence imposed on him by the bishops. The Pope indignantly replied, "Brother, by St. Peter you shall not so easily obtain absolution from us, after having inflicted such and so many injuries not only on the King of England himself, but also on the Church of Rome. We will, after deliberation with our brethren, decide how we are to punish such a rash fault."

Louis Invades England 1216

EUSTACE THE MONK, THE NOTORIOUS PIRATE OF THE English Channel, had provided Louis, son of the King of France, with a fleet of six hundred ships. With these Louis had landed his army safely on the isle of Thanet, on the 21st of May, 1216. The Pope had strictly forbidden Louis to invade England but Louis said he would settle this matter with the Pope later.

John was at Dover with a large army awaiting Louis' advance. Unfortunately for him, his army was composed almost entirely of French mercenaries. John knew from experience that they would desert to the French at the first opportunity, and because of this he did not dare attack Louis. So he retreated before the invasion, leaving Hubert de Burgh and a force of more than one hundred and forty knights to defend

Dover Castle. Hubert stoutly held the castle despite the almost constant attacks of the French besiegers.

Louis himself advanced on London where the jolly barons were waiting to receive him with a big celebration. Among them were several of John's principal nobles who had deserted him to take part in the welcome.

Louis invited all the English barons to join him, and several of them accepted the invitation. These merry turncoats did not know that Louis had promised all their estates to his French nobles and was planning to banish the English barons as traitors. When word of this leaked out the English barons were greatly disturbed, for they had been excommunicated by the Pope and did not dare to go back to John.

The barons were able to lay heavy siege to John's castle at Windsor, which, though it was defended by only sixty knights, resisted successfully all their fierce assaults.

Meanwhile, John with his army had slipped into the eastern provinces of Suffolk and Norfolk, burning crops and devastating the baronial estates. News of this so greatly discouraged the besiegers at Windsor that they abandoned the siege and, advancing to Cambridge, made a fruitless attempt to circumvent the King's army. But John slipped by them and marched northward to Lincoln where he raised the siege of his beleaguered castle.

The discouraged barons returned to London, stealing everything that was movable on the way. From London they proceeded to Louis at Dover where the siege was still in progress. For Louis had sworn he would not abandon the attack until the castle was taken and all the garrison hanged.

Restless and landless, John was marching to and fro across his torn and harried kingdom, burning and slaying but finding no place of rest where he might also find safety. He could trust neither his nobles nor the foreign mercenaries whom he must pay with the loot of his own kingdom. He carried this great treasure in a heavy wagon train wherever he went. Not only this treasure but all his personal possessions, wardrobe and the arms and munitions of war lumbered behind his troops in heavy carts and on pack horses. In the wake of his army he left the blackened waste of burnt harvest fields, smoking ruins of farms, manors, and looted churches. On all who fell into their power his savage soldiers inflicted fiendish tortures. But if the road behind was black and ruined the road ahead was darker still.

Each day the long column of horses and men filed northward. As they entered the town of Lynn the citizens poured out with cheers and banners to welcome them. The mayor and chief men brought the King rich presents, for despite his many cruelties John had favored the merchants and trading towns of the kingdom.

How the Earth and the Sea Overtook the King 1216

ALONG THE LOW EASTERN COAST WHERE THE WELL-stream River joins the sea was a vast wasteland called the Wash. It belonged neither to the sea nor to the land. For the tide in its eternal rhythm of ebb and flow changed it from one to the other continually. The shrill wailing of sea birds and the drifting fog and the smell of the sea haunted its melancholy reaches. Marsh glow flickered through the dusk and legends told of demons who waited in its bogs to pull travelers down into its slimy depths. Its shifting sands gave no footing for man or beast except for the slippery paths which crossed it and which were known only to a few of the marsh people.

John and his train drew rein and looked across the marshy waste. Impatiently the King ordered his horsemen forward and the cavalcade plunged into the quagmire. It was a desperate, floundering crossing but they finally found firm footing and rode on to Swineshead Abbey.

Slowly following the King was his baggage train of heavy carts and wagons loaded with his treasure and rich wardrobe, arms, tents, provisions and loot. When the train reached the Wash the heavy wagons plunged into the marsh for the King had ordered that they follow him without delay. Wagons, horses and oxen soon were sunk deep in the sand and ooze, foundering deeper where they could not find footing. As the tide began to rise they could go neither forward nor back. The cattle lowed dolefully and the horses neighed with fright as the sea and earth swallowed up the doomed train, for it seemed as if the earth opened in the midst of the waters, causing great whirlpools which sucked down man and beast until nothing remained.

When the news of this disaster reached the King he was overwhelmed. That night, burning with fever, he reached Swineshead Abbey, where the Abbot provided a feast for the royal glutton. He thirstily drank flagon after flagon of sweet cider, and gorged on the ripe peaches provided by his host.

Next day he rode on to Sleaford, hardly able to cling to his saddle. His men finally made a rough litter and laid him on it. For three days, in the Bishop of Lincoln's castle, the stricken King lay dying. He made his followers swear fealty to his eldest son, Henry, and sent word to William Marshal placing the boy in his keeping. He also sent letters to the sheriffs throughout the kingdom, commanding them to obey Henry as their lord. Last of all, the Abbot of Croxton Abbey administered the Eucharist to the dying King.

On the night of October 18, a terrible storm raged over the town. Amid its violence and blackness John Lackland passed away.

Next morning a monk entering the town at daybreak met the King's servants stealing out with the loot of the King's household. They had even robbed the dead King of his clothing.

In the morning the abbot came and embalmed and clothed the body. It is said that he took the King's heart, for John had bequeathed it to Croxton Abbey. Summoning a few of the King's men-at-arms, the bishop led the grim funeral procession across England to Worcester Abbey where the body was interred in the floor of the cathedral.

How Stephen Langton
Waited in Rome 1215

IN ROME STEPHEN LANGTON MEEKLY ACCEPTED THE confirmation of his suspension from office. He did not question his own guilt. He had aided the barons against the King for he could not in justice have done otherwise. He had neglected to announce the Pope's excommunication of the barons in England. His punishment was just. He had broken the rules and disobeyed orders. But he had kept faith with England and his conscience. He could do no less.

So he remained silent and waited. Perhaps it would be best, he reflected, if he were to retire from the world and live as a recluse, devoting himself to his books and prayer. This would be easy, even pleasant. It was a temptation. It seemed that all he had accomplished for freedom and justice in England was lost, for the Pope had annulled the Magna Charta and excommunicated the barons.

News came that civil war was drenching England in blood. It seemed that evil had triumphed, that King John as usual would win.

Praying and studying his Bible, Stephen Langton

read of the prophet hiding and trembling in the cave while the wind and the fire and the earthquake passed by, and of how, afterward, there came a great silence and the still small voice of Truth saying, "Go forth and stand upon the mount." Reading this, Stephen decided he would have faith and wait. Men who sought liberty were used to waiting. In England, as elsewhere, kings came and went. "The captains and the kings depart" but Truth remains. The Magna Charta would remain. It would always be there. It would stand through the ages. The people would remember it in times of persecution, and those who came after would turn to the charter saying, "These are our rights by the King's oath and seal."

So thought Stephen Langton, waiting in Rome the Eternal City, waiting for news from England. He was still Archbishop of Canterbury, primate of England, and work was there for him to do. He would wait and watch and pray. He would be ready to answer when the call came. He would return to his own.

Hubert de Burgh's Great Victory

THE GLITTERING PAGEANTRY OF THE BISHOPS AND nobles of England blazed about Henry, the nine-year-old boy who in a quavering voice repeated the solemn oaths required of a king of England. The Bishop of Winchester placed the heavy golden crown upon his head and anointed him king. Three times the shout rang out, "Long live the King!" William Marshal, his guardian, sent letters through all England enjoining obedience to Henry III, the newly crowned king. When it was known that Marshal had required the young King to approve the charter, there was a lift of the spirit throughout the land.

The news of John's death reached Louis while he was still besieging Dover Castle. He summoned Hubert de Burgh, who was still stubbornly holding it. "Your King is dead," Louis told De Burgh. "Surrender the castle to me and you shall have rich rewards and high office at my hands."

But Hubert looked him steadily in the eyes and replied that there was a rightful heir to England to whom he would be faithful. As for the castle, he would consult his knights about surrendering it. This he did, and "No surrender!" was their defiant answer.

Louis raised the siege and carried his attack to other castles. The rebel barons were now wavering between two masters as they watched Louis assign their castles and lands to his foreign lords.

William Marshal had assembled the king's army and, fired with patriotic fervor, had raised the siege of Lincoln and sent Louis' foreign troops fleeing to London. As the retreating Frenchmen passed through the English towns the citizens turned out with sword and spear and settled old accounts against the foreign invaders who had ravaged their lands.

In London Louis was greatly discomfited by this defeat. He sent to his father in France for reinforcements. But it was Louis' wife Blanche who summoned three hundred knights to go to the relief of her harassed husband. By this time Marshal's victorious army had advanced on London and laid siege to the city. Marshal also stationed troops along the southern coast to defend it from invaders.

After Louis had departed from under their walls the starved defenders of Dover Castle had sallied out and looted the countryside of whatever was edible after the French had taken their toll. Hubert de Burgh and his lean knights began to put flesh on their bare ribs again.

When news reached Hubert that a French fleet was on its way to England, he immediately urged the barons to join him and sail forth to destroy it. But the barons declined, saying scornfully they were neither sailors, pirates nor fishermen.

Hubert had defended the gate of England too long and too well to be disheartened by this cowardice on the part of the nobles. He said his prayers and, assuming the boldness of a lion, assembled his staunchest knights and launched forth to meet the enemy. He left Dover Castle in charge of a trusted lieutenant, saying, "If they should make me prisoner, let them hang me rather than that I should surrender the castle to any Frenchmen, for it is the key to England."

The English sailors were sea dogs of the Cinque Ports, and they were eager for a brush with their old enemy Eustace the monk, that most disgraceful man and wicked pirate who was in command of the French fleet.

With superb seamanship the English maneuvered so as to strike the French galleys from the rear. Throwing out grappling irons, some of the English boarded the enemy ships and with their axes cut down masts and rigging while their bowmen rained showers of arrows on the decks. Other Englishmen in ships to windward threw clouds of lime dust in the air, burning the throats and eyes of the French sailors. English galleys with iron beaks stove in the sides of the enemy ships and agile boarders made holes in the bottoms so that they sank.

The action was swift and fierce and the victory so complete that the entire French fleet was taken and towed triumphantly into Dover harbor. After a long search Eustace the monk was dragged forth from the hold of one of the ships. He offered a large sum in the hope that his life might be spared, swearing he would faithfully serve the English king. But Richard, an illegitimate son of King John, cried, "Never again, wicked traitor, shall you deceive anyone with your false promises!" And drawing his sword, he cut off Eustace's head.

The Treaty of Lambeth

AFTER THIS WILLIAM MARSHAL, THE KING'S GUARDIAN
and regent, advanced upon London and so thoroughly
did he shut up the city that for lack of necessary provisions and supplies Louis and all his host were compelled to ask for terms. Louis swore that he would
immediately leave England with all his followers,
that he would never again return with evil designs,
and that he would give up all the lands and castles in
England which he had seized.

The young King of England swore to restore all
the rights and liberties to his barons according to the
great charter his father had granted. All the prisoners who had been taken on both sides were set free
with great joy, and after these things were done each
and all gave one another the kiss of peace.

This was ever after called the great Treaty of Lambeth, and at this time all England was freed from cruel invaders, and the bitter strife that had torn the kingdom for many years ceased. Stephen Langton came again from Rome and was Archbishop of Canterbury, William Marshal was the King's regent and guardian, and Hubert de Burgh was justiciar of the realm. These three were true men as well as the King's councilors, and they would guard well the rights and liberties of all.

Louis received five thousand pounds to meet his necessities, and then under the conduct of the grand marshal he went with all speed to the sea coast, and thence, in lasting ignominy, crossed to France.

All things being thus set in order, William Marshal mounted his white charger and gave the signal that his liegemen should follow. The heralds sounded three fanfares on their silver trumpets, the wind fluttered the bright banners, the sun danced on helmet and mail, and the great cavalcade rode inland over the long downs toward London.

"*No freeman shall be taken or imprisoned, or disseized, or outlawed, or banished, or anyways destroyed, nor will we pass upon him, nor will we send upon him, unless by the lawful judgment of his peers, or by the law of the land. We will sell to no man, we will not deny to any man, either justice or right.*"

MAGNA CHARTA
1215

PART FOUR 🙰
CHILDREN OF
THE MAGNA CHARTA

Milestones that have marked the long road
from Magna Charta

And the chief captain answered,
With a great sum obtained I this freedom.
And Paul said, But I was free born.

(The Acts of the Apostles)

How Charters Came to America

Although English kings were required at their coronation to swear to abide by the rights of the Magna Charta, they were sometimes very reluctant to do so and were determined to keep on ruling by their own personal will, unrestricted by the charter.

Some of them believed this mistaken notion was the "divine right of kings."

The kings who tried to rule by this theory caused themselves and their people a lot of trouble and bloodshed. It finally cost King Charles I his handsome, willful head. Even after so grim a warning kings persisted in this same error.

King James the Second was one of these, and because of it he had to leave England and his throne permanently. And George the Third, who still believed in the personal authority of kings, lost a large part of North America because of this mistake.

This interesting and valuable continent had been claimed in part by English explorers and discoverers for their sovereigns, and so became the property of the crown according to traditional English law.

Therefore when English subjects began to settle this land it was necessary for them to get charters from the crown granting them the right to occupy the land in perpetual tenancy and to set up a form of government and of course to pay taxes into the royal treasury.

Enterprising individuals and companies obtained their rights to settle certain sections of this new dominion by charters granted to them by their sovereign. In time thirteen American colonies were established and obtained their precious royal charters. These they valued highly because by them they were secured in whatever rights and liberties they possessed, as well as the obligations they incurred, by the grant and authority of the crown.

The Indians did not have any charters to prove their rights and liberties, but the colonists very generously gave them a few red shirts and lots of very bad whiskey to sign papers saying that of their own free will they sold all their rights to the land to the white people forever. This, it was thought at the time, made everything right and legal for everyone.

The Mayflower Compact

*"We whose names are underwritten . . . having
undertaken for the glory of God and advancement
of the Christian faith . . . a voyage to plant the first
colony in the northern parts of Virginia. . . ."*

From the *Mayflower* Compact

IN MID OCEAN IN THE NORTH ATLANTIC IN OCTOBER,
1620, a little ship rose and fell, her great brown sails
bulging under a stiff breeze.

Under a gray sky the heaving waters stretched wild
and bleak to the horizon's rim. The *Mayflower* lifted
with a splash of foam from her bows on the rise of a
heavy sea and slid down the long backs of the gray-
green mountains of tossing waters. So it had been for
weeks.

There were one hundred and two passengers aboard
besides the crew. Among them was a congregation of
English Separatists (or Pilgrims) from Leyden, Holland. There were also adventurers and the riffraff of
the London slums and the hard-bitten British seamen.

The captain grimly watched the wind and the sea
keeping the ship driving ever westward like the master craftsman of the sea that he was. Though he did
not know it, he was steering the course of history as
well, and on his skill depended the lives of everyone
on the ship.

The Pilgrims pored over their Bibles and joined in
the prayers and hymns. The seamen swore horribly,

spat scornfully and stepped lively at the captain's commands. The food was bad and the drinking water foul. A Pilgrim wife bore a baby. He was named Oceanus.

A passenger died. The great main beam of the ship cracked under the force of the sea. A heavy prop, or stanchion, was improvised for support and the danger averted.

Landfall was made on November 11, after a nine weeks' voyage. It was the tip of Cape Cod, far to the north of the passengers' destination. They turned south but the heavy weather and the lateness of the season decided them to turn back. The *Mayflower* dropped anchor just inside the fishhook point of Cape Cod. This land was outside the jurisdiction of English government and law, and the rougher element was saying wildly that they would recognize no law. But the majority of the company were law-abiding folk with the Anglo-Saxon instinct for law and order. In the crowded cabin of the *Mayflower* they drew up the brief *Mayflower* Compact promising obedience to the laws of their own making. They were not thinking of democracy but of majority rule and law and order, of unity and decent living in the struggle for survival with the wilderness. The cornerstone of the new world their hands would make would be this compact for law and order with justice and peace for all.

Forty-one men signed the document, the first names

on the bright scroll of American liberty—John Carver, William Bradford, William Brewster, Edward Winslow, Miles Standish and John Alden among them.

The *Mayflower* Compact was the small seed of democracy dropped in dark soil of the wilderness to be nourished in faith and watered with blood, growing through the years into a mighty tree, its branches outspread to the world bearing the bright fruit of liberty.

The Mayflower Compact

(Signed in the cabin of the *Mayflower* November, 1620.)

In ye name of God, Amen.

> We whose names are underwriten,
> the loyall subjects of our
> dread soveraigne Lord, King James,
> by ye grace of God, of Great Britaine,
> France, & Ireland, king,
> defender of Ye faith, &c.,
> Haveing undertaken, for ye glorie of God,
> and advancemente of ye Christian faith,
> and the honour of our King & countrie,
> a voyage to plant ye first colonie

in ye Northerne parts of Virginia
Doe by these presents solemnly &
                              mutually
in ye presence of God, and one of
                              another,
covenant & combine ourselves togeather
into a civill body politick, for our
better ordering & preservation &
                              furtherance
of ye ends aforesaid; and by vertue hereof
to enacte, constitute, and frame
such just & equall lawes, ordinances,
                              acts,
constitutions, & offices, from time to
                              time,
as shall be thought most meete and convenient
for ye generall good of ye Colonie:
unto which we promise all due submission
and obedience.
    In witness whereof we have hereunto
subscribed our names at Cap-Codd
ye 11 of November in ye year of ye
                              raigne
of our soveraigne Lord, King James,
of England, France, & Ireland
ye eighteenth and of Scotland ye
                              fiftie fourth.
Ano: Dom. 1620.

The American Colonists
Wrote a Charter ^{July 4}

THERE WAS SOMETHING ABOUT THE LAND AND AIR OF America that made the people who came here want more freedom. Soon the colonists decided they wanted more liberties than were set forth in their royal charters. One day in 1776 they got together and wrote a new charter of their own. It began:

"WE HOLD THESE TRUTHS TO BE SELF EVIDENT: THAT ALL MEN ARE CREATED EQUAL; THAT THEY ARE ENDOWED BY THEIR CREATOR WITH CERTAIN UNALIENABLE RIGHTS."

This was something absolutely new in charters. No charter had ever said this before. It was controversial, it was radical, it was very dangerous. It was a DECLARATION OF INDEPENDENCE.

It went on to state some unpleasant "facts to be submitted to a candid world" about "the present King of Great Britain." The King was not even asked to sign this charter.

But it was signed.

It was signed by the people themselves, thusly:

"WE, THEREFORE, THE REPRESENTATIVES OF THE UNITED STATES OF AMERICA, IN GENERAL CONGRESS ASSEMBLED."

[138]

It concluded by stating:

·"AND FOR THE SUPPORT OF THIS DECLARATION,
WITH A FIRM RELIANCE ON THE PROTECTION OF
DIVINE PROVIDENCE,
WE MUTUALLY PLEDGE TO EACH OTHER OUR LIVES,
OUR FORTUNES AND OUR SACRED HONOR."

And the people have kept their pledge and have paid the stated price in God's plenty more than once.

The pledge still stands and the price is the same.

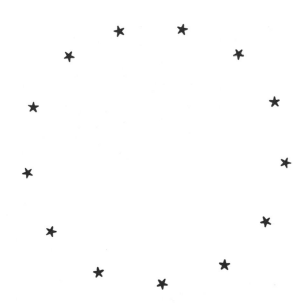

The Times That Try Men's Souls

He that would make his own liberty secure must guard even his enemy from oppression; for if he violates this duty he establishes a precedent that will reach to himself.

Thomas Paine

THOMAS PAINE WAS BORN IN ENGLAND OF QUAKER parents and had grown up in the poverty and misery of the English industrial towns. He knew the life of the slums which Hogarth had so grimly drawn in his pictures of "Gin Lane" and "Beer Alley." He had come to Philadelphia at the age of thirty-seven with letters from Benjamin Franklin who had said, "Where is Liberty, there is my country." Paine had retorted, "Where Liberty is not, there is mine." He joined the revolutionaries.

In 1776 Paine published a pamphlet called "Common Sense" rousing the colonies to independence. He followed this with "The Crisis," that called up visions of ragged men marching in wind and snow to the fifes and drums of Revolution in the words "These are the times that try men's souls. The summer soldier and the sunshine patriot will, in this crisis, shrink from the service of their country; but he that stands it now deserves the love and thanks of man and woman."

His phrases had fire and power that called up people's armies in a time of revolution, and with his pen he turned over the world. He was the first to use those majestic words, "The United States of America." He advocated women's rights, abolition of slavery, old-age pensions, he foresaw a United Nations.

He was always on the side of the poor, the weak, and the underdog. He wrote, "I defend the cause of the poor, of the manufacturers, of the tradesman, of the farmer, and all those on whom the real burden of taxes fall—but above all I defend the cause of humanity." After taking part in the French Revolution he returned to America in 1802 and spent the last seven years of his life in New York. Of him Gamaliel Bradford has justly written:

"Every American ought to be grateful to him as one of the active founders of the United States of America."

"In Order to Form a More Perfect Union" ^{Sept. 17 1787}

THIRTEEN YEARS AFTER THE DECLARATION OF INDE-dependence the United States, which were not so united at the time, reluctantly got together and wrote another charter. It began:

"WE, THE PEOPLE OF THE UNITED STATES, IN ORDER TO FORM A MORE PERFECT UNION . . . DO ORDAIN AND ESTABLISH THIS CONSTITUTION FOR THE UNITED STATES OF AMERICA."

The English king was not even mentioned in this charter. The new sovereign was announced as "WE THE PEOPLE."

"WE"—the sassy, rambunctious people—were speaking out and taking over and saying, "This is the way WE want it, and this is the way it is going to be—a government of the people, for the people, by the people.

"WE made it. WE like it. It is going to work and it does!"

Then, just to make sure that they were not giving away all their rights and liberties even to their own government, they added ten amendments. They were

[142]

added somewhat like the tail to a kite, so that when dangerous winds blew the kite would not take a dive and the people lose some of their freedoms.

These ten amendments are called "THE BILL OF RIGHTS."

Even so, there was something left out.

Jefferson, in his draft of the Declaration of Independence, had denounced slavery, but the Continental Congress thought the subject too controversial at the time, and so they had struck it out. The Constitution said nothing about the thousands of Negro slaves who had no rights in this new land of liberty. The people still had to learn that a nation cannot remain permanently half slave and half free.

It took a terrible civil war to get a few words on this subject added to the Constitution. These are:

"NEITHER SLAVERY NOR INVOLUNTARY SERVITUDE, EXCEPT AS A PUNISHMENT FOR CRIME WHEREOF THE PARTY SHALL HAVE BEEN DULY CONVICTED, SHALL EXIST WITHIN THE UNITED STATES, OR ANY PLACE SUBJECT TO THEIR JURISDICTION."

(Amendment XIII, Section I.)

"This Country...Belongs to the People." March 4 1861

FROM THE FLAG-DRAPED PLATFORM ON THE EAST STEPS of the Capitol and beneath its unfinished dome, Lincoln delivered his first inaugural address. In this address he majestically said:

"A majority held in restraint by constitutional checks and limitations, and always changing easily with deliberate changes of popular opinions and sentiments is the only true sovereign of a free people.

"This country, with its institutions, belongs to the people who inhabit it. Whenever they shall grow weary of the existing government, they can exercise their constitutional right of amending it, or their revolutionary right to dismember or overthrow it.

"Why should there not be a patient confidence in the ultimate justice of the people? Is there any better or equal hope, in the world?

"By the frame of government under which we live, this same people have wisely given their public servants but little power for mischief; and have, with equal wisdom, provided for the return of that little to their own hands at very short intervals. While the people retain their virtue and vigilance, no administration, by any extreme of wickedness or folly, can very seriously injure the government in the short space of four years."

But it was not directly by an act of the only true sovereign of a free people that the first great step to free slaves was taken in the United States. It was "by virtue of the power in me vested as Commander-in-Chief of the Army and Navy of the United States in time of actual armed rebellion against authority and government of the United States" that Lincoln issued the final Emancipation Proclamation which stated:

"THAT ON THE FIRST DAY OF JANUARY, IN THE YEAR OF OUR LORD ONE THOUSAND EIGHT HUNDRED AND SIXTY THREE, ALL PERSONS HELD AS SLAVES WITHIN ANY STATE, OR DESIGNATED PART OF A STATE, THE PEOPLE WHEREOF SHALL THEN BE IN REBELLION AGAINST THE UNITED STATES, SHALL BE THEN, THENCE-FORWARD AND FOREVER FREE. . . ."

The concluding paragraph stated:

"AND UPON THIS ACT SINCERELY BELIEVED TO BE AN ACT OF JUSTICE, WARRANTED BY THE CONSTITUTION UPON MILITARY NECESSITY, I INVOKE THE CONSIDERATE JUDGMENT OF MANKIND, AND THE GRACIOUS FAVOR OF ALMIGHTY GOD."

The President's Proclamation liberated only those slaves in states which were in rebellion against the government.

The total abolition of slavery was proposed in the

thirteenth amendment to the Constitution. This amendment was submitted to the states by Congress for ratification January 13, 1865. It required the approval of three-fourths of the legislatures of the thirty-six states of the Union at that time. Georgia was the twenty-seventh, the last necessary state to ratify, her legislature so voting on December 6, 1865. On December 18 following, Secretary of State Seward certified the amendment.

Thus the dreadful curse of human slavery was legally abolished forever in the United States.

Women Are Citizens 1920

ONE RAINY DAY IN THE YEAR 1872 A YOUNG WOMAN was sitting in a rocking chair in Rochester, New York, reading the Constitution. When she came to the Fifteenth Amendment she read:

"THE RIGHTS OF CITIZENS OF THE UNITED STATES TO VOTE SHALL NOT BE ABRIDGED ON ACCOUNT OF RACE, COLOR, OR PREVIOUS CONDITION OF SERVITUDE."

She thought about this awhile and then she said, "Women are citizens of the United States. Why can't they vote?"

Her name was Susan B. Anthony.

When registration day came around, Susan and a number of her women friends went down to the local barber shop and said to the registrar, "We are going to vote. We want to register."

"No," said the man. "It's not legal."

"Yes," said Susan. "We're citizens, aren't we?"

"Yes," said the man. "I reckon you are."

"Then hand me the pen," said Susan.

"No," said the man. "I'm telling you it's not legal."

"Oh, yes, it is. According to Amendment Fifteen, Article One of the Constitution of the United States it is legal," she said, showing the registrar the document. "Hand me that pen."

Men in barber shops are not usually very good at arguing with women; so Susan and her friends were the first women in the United States to register as voters.

On Election Day they went to the polls and voted. They were all arrested. Susan was tried and found guilty. She was fined one hundred dollars, but the sheriff did not dare to collect it, though he tried in a half-hearted sort of way.

For the next fifty years there was a lot of argument about women's right to vote. In 1920 Congress adopted the nineteenth amendment to the Constitution, which said quite simply and finally, "THE RIGHTS OF CITIZENS OF THE UNITED STATES TO VOTE SHALL NOT BE DENIED OR ABRIDGED BY THE UNITED STATES OR ANY STATE ON ACCOUNT OF SEX."

In the presidential election that year 6,000,000 women voted for the first time in the United States.

So far, twenty-one amendments have been added to the Constitution.

The Constitution is a living charter that grows in wise, slow ways by the will of the people.

A New Magna Charta for the American Republics

The First International Conference of American States Washington, D.C. 1910.

When we speak of "America" we mean, of course, that smaller half of the North American Continent which is occupied by the United States. But on the maps America is both of the continents—North and South—which together comprise the Western Hemisphere.

Every schoolboy and girl knows this. But we need to remember as never before that the United States is not all of America and that America means something a great deal bigger than just the United States. In the Americas, North and South, are twenty-one republics including the United States, and their peoples are all Americans.

When the Nazi armies moved victoriously across Europe, the peoples of the Western Hemisphere were suddenly forced to think very fast about not only national defense, but something bigger—Western Hemisphere defense.

[149]

The ideal of inter-American cooperation was not exactly new. Simón Bolívar, the great South American liberator, had called a Congress of American Republics which met at Panama in 1826. This Congress signed a Treaty of Confederation which provided for collective security, for a "Perpetual Union, League and Confederation" and for arbitration of inter-American disputes; in effect, a League of Nations of the New World.

But the New World was not yet ready for Bolívar's noble idea. It was not until 1899 that another American of large vision, James G. Blaine, took definite steps toward inter-American cooperation.

As a result of Blaine's efforts the First International Conference of American States was held at Washington, D. C., in 1899–90. Among other useful things this conference created The International Union of American Republics and the Commercial Bureau of American Republics. (The names were changed to the Pan American Union in 1910.)

These agencies became so useful in furnishing information and creating mutual understanding that in 1910 a handsome marble building, "The House of the Americas," was erected in Washington, D. C. as a permanent home for the Pan American Union at a cost of one million dollars. Most of this was donated by Andrew Carnegie. Every visitor to Washington would do well to enter its hospitable doors for, like the United Nations buildings in New York, it is an inspiring landmark on the road toward international good will and understanding among peoples.

Since the first session in 1910 ten meetings of the International Conference of American Republics have been held (as of 1956). At each of them practical steps have been taken expanding cooperation and strengthening security among its members. The impact of two shattering world wars has only served to strengthen these ties.

At the ninth meeting of the International Conference, held at Bogotá, Colombia in 1948, The Organization of American States was established. Its charter was signed by 21 American republics representing 264,000,000 people. The charter affirmed their determination "to achieve an order and peace and justice, to promote their solidarity, to strengthen their collaboration, and to defend their sovereignty, their territorial integrity and their independence."

These are not merely fine words. The Organization of American States, with cooperation as its key note, has planned and is carrying out active programs for improvement in health, housing, agriculture, trade, education, and child welfare, as well as cultural relations through art, music and travel.

Since 1950, under its program of technical cooperation, technicians from all the American republics have been trained in new methods of farming, teaching, nursing and other activities vital to human welfare, and these have been sent back to their respective countries to train others in new techniques. Millions of people in backward areas are being lifted out of ignorance, poverty and disease through the agencies of the O. A. S.

Young as it is, the O. A. S. is one of the oldest international organizations in the world. It has been said "the story of peace in the Western Hemisphere is the story of the Organization of American States." (From *Pan Americanism at Work,* published by Pan American Union, Washington, D. C.)

April 14th has been designated as "Pan American Day" throughout the Americas, for it was on this day in 1890 that the Pan American Union was established. As we grow to value the peace, unity and security of the Western Hemisphere this day will be more generally celebrated. At the close of the First International Conference of American States at Washington, D. C., its chairman, Secretary of State Blaine, said, calling the world's attention "to the deliberate, confident, solemn dedication of two great continents to peace, and to the prosperity which peace has for its foundation,

"WE HOLD UP THIS NEW MAGNA CHARTA, WHICH ABOLISHES WAR AND SUBSTITUTES ARBITRATION BETWEEN THE AMERICAN REPUBLICS, AS THE FIRST AND GREAT FRUIT OF THE INTERNATIONAL AMERICAN CONFERENCE."

The Covenant of the League of Nations 1920-1946

AFTER FOUR TERRIBLE YEARS, THE FIRST WORLD WAR
—the war "to make the world safe for democracy"—
was over. That was in 1918. For a brief bright moment the people of the allied nations rejoiced in the
hope that the war to end all wars had been won.

During the peace conference a Commission on the
League of Nations met to draw up a covenant based
on President Wilson's Fourteen Points.

Point Fourteen provided that "a general associa-
tion of nations should be formed on the basis of
covenants designed to create mutual guarantees of
the political independence and territorial integrity of
states, large and small equally."

The Covenant was inserted in the Treaty of Ver-
sailles and other peace treaties so that every nation
signing them automatically subscribed to the Covenant. Twenty-seven nations became members of the
League of Nations. The United States did not sub-
scribe to it. The League met twice a year, usually at
Geneva, and continued its existence for twenty-six

years. As Russia was never invited to join, and the United States refused to join, the League was hopelessly handicapped from the start.

The League made no attempt to defend China against Japanese aggression in 1931. When Franco attacked the new Republic of Spain in 1934, the nations of Europe passively watched the tanks and planes of Hitler and Mussolini try out the new techniques of modern warfare.

When Haile Selassie, Emperor of Ethiopia, appeared in person before the League and pleaded for aid against the Italian invasion of his country in 1935, the League denounced the invasion as "an act of war against a member of the League," but did nothing effective about it. As a result, Italy annexed Ethiopia.

The League proved to be ineffectual to prevent war and held its last meeting in 1946. Andrew Boyd has written of the League of Nations, "Certainly it has failed. But the League idea has not failed. Reformed and revitalized, it is the idea behind the United Nations.

"In justice to Wilson and his fellow pioneers, it must be said that their Covenant represents an advance in the development of world organization so huge and so unprecedented that it will inevitably take its place as a turning point in human history." (*The United Nations Organization Handbook by Andrew Boyd, Pilot Press, Inc., N. Y., 1946.*)

The Four Essential Freedoms

By January, 1941, Britain stood with her back to the wall, facing Nazi invasion. The disaster and the miracle of Dunkirk had saved the remnants of Britain's army but the Germans held Boulogne and looked across the channel to the white cliffs of Dover, even as Napoleon had done over a hundred years before. At that time the Little Corporal had said somewhat wistfully, "Let us be masters of the channel for six hours and we shall be masters of the world." Churchill, announcing to the world that Britain would never surrender to another corporal, had said, "Let us therefore brace ourselves that, if the British Empire and its Commonwealth last for a thousand years, men will say, 'This was England's finest hour!' "

In America the great debate was going on: "Shall America go in or keep out?" "Shall America stand on the side line waiting as the free nations of Europe go down one by one, waiting her turn to meet the Nazi Frankenstein alone?" "Or shall America take freedom's side and spend treasure and blood, to the

[155]

last drop if need be, that Hitler's thousand years shall never come to pass?" Many in Congress wanted to keep America out, to keep neutral, or even make peace with the Nazis on the basis of a world half slave, half free. "Let Europe fight her own wars," such people said. "Let Britain sink."

The President had called on the people to make America the arsenal of democracy, urging that, if we furnished the tools of war to those fighting the aggressors, there would be no need for an American expeditionary force. Only Britain stood between America and the seemingly invincible Nazi hordes. It was the zero hour.

On January 6, 1941, President Roosevelt stood at the Speaker's desk addressing a joint session of Congress. He denounced appeasement and called again for all-out aid to Britain and all nations resisting the Axis.

At the end of the speech he spoke of the future, envisioning a new world order of peace and freedom beyond the blackness of the present hour. Listening over their radios, the world's troubled millions took heart as they heard these words:

"In the future days, which we seek to make secure, we look forward to a world founded upon four essential freedoms.

"The first is freedom of speech and expression—everywhere in the world.

"The second is freedom of every person to worship God in his own way—everywhere in the world.

"The third is freedom from want—which, translated into world terms, means economic understanding which will secure to every nation a healthy peacetime life for its inhabitants—everywhere in the world.

"The fourth is freedom from fear—which, translated into world terms, means a world-wide reduction of armaments to such a point and in such a thorough fashion that no nation will be in a position to commit an act of physical aggression against any neighbor—anywhere in the world.

"That is no vision of a distant millennium. It is a definite basis for a kind of world attainable in our own time and generation. That kind of world is the very antithesis of the so-called new order of tyranny which the dictators seek to create with the crash of a bomb.

"To that new order we oppose the greater conception—the moral order. A good society is able to face schemes of world domination and foreign revolutions alike without fear.

"Since the beginning of our American history we have been engaged in change—in a perpetual peaceful revolution—a revolution which goes on steadily, quietly adjusting itself to changing conditions—without the concentration camp or the quick-lime in the ditch. The world order which we seek is the cooperation of free countries, working together in a friendly, civilized society.

"This Nation has placed its destiny in the hands and heads and hearts of its millions of free men and women; and its faith in freedom under the guidance of God. Freedom means the supremacy of human rights everywhere. Our support goes to those who struggle to gain those rights or keep them. Our strength is in our unity of purpose.

"To that high concept there can be no end save victory."

The Atlantic Charter

In early August, 1941, Washington, D. C. was agog with mystery.

President Roosevelt had disappeared on a fishing trip off the Maine coast and Prime Minister Winston Churchill had vanished from London.

It was no time for anybody, much less the President, to go fishing!

For two years, England had been the target for terrible bombing by the Germans. Churchill had called this ordeal England's finest hour because of the magnificent courage with which the English people fought back the aggressor. From the Arctic to the Black Sea Hitler's armies in Russia were pushing back the Stalin Line. In July, Great Britain and Russia had pledged mutual aid in the Anglo-Russian Agreement. The United States was sending the tools of war to both countries. She had announced that she was the arsenal of democracy and was, herself, desperately arming. The great debate between the isolationists and the interventionists raged in Congress and throughout the country.

Every day the headlines told of the terrible destruction done by the German U-boats, the wolf packs of the Atlantic, on the flanks of the convoy fleets. In May, the President had told the people that the rate of Nazi sinkings of merchant ships was more than twice the combined British and American output of replacements.

At Placenta Bay off the Newfoundland coast the United States cruiser *Augusta* and her escort lay at anchor, waiting. Aboard the cruiser was President Roosevelt.

On the morning of August 9, at 4 a.m., the battleship *Prince of Wales* majestically came to anchor within hailing distance. She had brought Winston Churchill across the perilous sub-infested North Atlantic to this prearranged secret rendezvous. By telephone, the two men had frequently spoken across thousands of miles of ocean but they had never met before. The Prime Minister set foot on the deck of the *Augusta* and said to the President: "I have brought you a letter from His Majesty, the King of England."

Stocky, ruddy Winston Churchill, the physical and spiritual impersonation of Great Britain, and the tall, lame President, with his chin held high, found it easy to become friends, to exchange ideas, and to form a warm understanding, one that strengthened the blood ties of the two great democracies.

They were met to pool the total resources of their countries, and something more besides—to voice the hopes of humanity, in time of peril, for peace and liberty with justice.

On August 12th, in the cabin of the *Augusta,* the two men approved the final draft of the eight points of the Atlantic Charter.

The Atlantic Charter came as a surprise to people reading their newspapers on the morning of August 14, 1941; it brought a lift of encouragement and new determination.

A week later the President, speaking before Congress, said: "No society of the world organized under the announced principles could survive without these freedoms which are a part of the whole freedom for which we strive."

And Churchill told his people: "When I looked upon that densely packed congregation of fighting men of the same language, of the same faith, of the same fundamental laws, of the same ideals, and now to a large extent the same interests, and certainly in different degrees facing the same dangers, it swept across me that here was the only hope, but also the sure hope, of saving the world from measureless degradation . . . and so we came back across the ocean waves, uplifted in spirit, fortified in resolve."

The Atlantic Charter August 14, 1941

THE PRESIDENT OF THE UNITED STATES OF AMERICA AND THE PRIME MINISTER, MR. CHURCHILL, REPRESENTING HIS MAJESTY'S GOVERNMENT OF THE UNITED KINGDOM, BEING MET TOGETHER, DEEM IT RIGHT TO MAKE KNOWN CERTAIN COMMON PRINCIPLES IN THE NATIONAL POLICIES OF THEIR RESPECTIVE COUNTRIES ON WHICH THEY BASE THEIR HOPES FOR A BETTER FUTURE FOR THE WORLD.

1. THEIR COUNTRIES SEEK NO AGGRANDISEMENT, TERRITORIAL OR OTHER.

2. THEY DESIRE TO SEE NO TERRITORIAL CHANGES THAT DO NOT ACCORD WITH THE FREELY EXPRESSED WISHES OF THE PEOPLE CONCERNED.

3. THEY RESPECT THE RIGHTS OF ALL PEOPLES TO CHOOSE THE FORM OF GOVERNMENT UNDER WHICH THEY WILL LIVE; AND THEY WISH TO SEE SOVEREIGN RIGHTS AND SELF-GOVERNMENT RESTORED TO THOSE WHO HAVE BEEN FORCIBLY DEPRIVED OF THEM.

4. THEY WILL ENDEAVOUR, WITH DUE RESPECT FOR THEIR EXISTING OBLIGATIONS, TO FURTHER THE ENJOYMENT BY ALL STATES, GREAT OR SMALL, VICTOR OR VANQUISHED, OF ACCESS, ON EQUAL TERMS, TO ALL TRADE AND TO THE RAW MATERIALS OF THE WORLD WHICH ARE NEEDED FOR THEIR ECONOMIC PROSPERITY.

5. THEY DESIRE TO BRING ABOUT THE FULLEST COLLABORATION BETWEEN ALL NATIONS IN THE ECONOMIC

FIELD WITH THE OBJECT OF SECURING, FOR ALL, IM-
PROVED LABOUR STANDARDS, ECONOMIC ADVANCEMENT
AND SOCIAL SECURITY.

6. AFTER THE FINAL DESTRUCTION OF THE NAZI
TYRANNY, THEY HOPE TO SEE ESTABLISHED A PEACE
WHICH WILL AFFORD TO ALL NATIONS THE MEANS OF
DWELLING IN SAFETY WITHIN THEIR OWN BOUNDARIES,
AND WHICH WILL AFFORD ASSURANCE THAT ALL THE
MEN IN ALL THE LANDS MAY LIVE OUT THEIR LIVES IN
FREEDOM FROM FEAR AND WANT.

7. SUCH A PEACE SHOULD ENABLE ALL MEN TO TRA-
VERSE THE HIGH SEAS AND OCEANS WITHOUT HINDRANCE.

8. THEY BELIEVE THAT ALL OF THE NATIONS OF THE
WORLD, FOR REALISTIC AS WELL AS SPIRITUAL REASONS,
MUST COME TO THE ABANDONMENT OF THE USE OF
FORCE, SINCE NO FUTURE PEACE CAN BE MAINTAINED
IF LAND, SEA OR AIR ARMAMENTS CONTINUE TO BE
EMPLOYED BY NATIONS WHICH THREATEN, OR MAY
THREATEN, AGGRESSION OUTSIDE OF THEIR FRONTIERS.
THEY BELIEVE, PENDING THE ESTABLISHMENT OF A
WIDER AND PERMANENT SYSTEM OF GENERAL SECURITY,
THAT THE DISARMAMENT OF SUCH NATIONS IS ESSEN-
TIAL. THEY WILL LIKEWISE AID AND ENCOURAGE ALL
OTHER PRACTICABLE MEASURES WHICH WILL LIGHTEN
FOR PEACE-LOVING PEOPLE THE CRUSHING BURDEN OF
ARMAMENTS.

FRANKLIN D. ROOSEVELT
WINSTON S. CHURCHILL

[163]

The Declaration by the
United Nations

ON SUNDAY AFTERNOON, DECEMBER 7, 1941, THE
people of the United States, dozing over the comics,
suddenly dropped their newspapers as they listened
to their radios abruptly announce the terrible news
of the bombing of Pearl Harbor. In twenty minutes'
time most of the Pacific fleet had been sent to the
bottom by Japanese planes and submarines.

America, like Europe, learned in that terrible moment how modern warfare strikes without the for-
mality of polite declarations of war. The people of
the United States, suddenly blasted into the war,
awoke to the realities. The great debate was suddenly
ended.

The next day in a six-minute speech President
Roosevelt tersely told a joint session of Congress:

"Yesterday, December 7, 1941—a date which will
live in infamy—the United States of America was
suddenly and deliberately attacked by naval and air
forces of the Empire of Japan. . . .

"Last night Japanese forces attacked Hong Kong.

"Last night Japanese forces attacked Guam.

[164]

"Last night Japanese forces attacked the Philippine Islands.

"This morning the Japanese attacked Midway Island. . . .

"I ask that the Congress declare that since the unprovoked and dastardly attack by Japan on Sunday, December 7th, a state of war has existed between the United States and the Japanese Empire."

Later, over the radio, the President spoke to the people: "We are now in the midst of a war, not for conquest, not for vengeance, but for a world in which this Nation, and all that this Nation represents, will be safe for our children. . . . We are going to win this war and we are going to win the peace that follows."

Still later, reporting on the progress of the war: "From Berlin, Rome and Tokyo we have been described as a nation of weaklings—'playboys'—who would hire British soldiers, or Russian soldiers, or Chinese soldiers to do our fighting for us.

"Let them repeat that now!

"Let them tell that to General MacArthur and his men.

"Let them tell that to the sailors who today are hitting hard in the far waters of the Pacific.

"Let them tell that to the boys in the Flying Fortresses.

"Let them tell that to the Marines!"

On New Year's Day, 1942, four men sat around a table in the White House. They represented the "Big Four"—Great Britain, the U.S.S.R., China, and the United States—comprising over half the population of the world. They were signing a brief document, a declaration subscribing to the purposes and principles of the Atlantic Charter, all pledging to employ their full resources to the struggle in which they were engaged, and never to make a separate peace. The pact was called a *Declaration by the United Nations*. This was the first time the designation "United Nations" was officially used. President Roosevelt had inserted the term to imply something more enduring than wartime allies. It suggested a continuing unity for enduring peace, the way to a new kind of world.

The men who signed this brief document were: Franklin D. Roosevelt, Winston Churchill, Maxim Litvinov and T. V. Soong.

Next day, at the office of the Assistant Secretary of State, the representatives of twenty-two other nations signed the document. Eventually it bore signatures representing forty-six nations. Behind the Atlantic Charter now stood the greatest union of power in the history of the world. In the world's darkest hour liberty-loving peoples had combined as the "United Nations."

The United Nations Charter June 26 1945

ON THE FLAG-DECORATED STAGE OF THE SAN FRAN-
cisco Opera House the representatives of fifty nations
had signed the United Nations Charter. For two
months they had hammered it out around the conference tables. They had spoken freely and often
disagreed. "But when we disagreed we tried again
and then again until we ended by reconciling the
differences between us."

The opening words of the Charter seemed
weighted with the blood and tears of all the wars of
the world:

"WE, THE PEOPLES OF THE UNITED NATIONS, DETER-
MINED TO SAVE SUCCEEDING GENERATIONS FROM THE
SCOURGE OF WAR, WHICH TWICE IN OUR LIFETIME HAS
BROUGHT UNTOLD SORROW TO MANKIND, AND

TO REAFFIRM FAITH IN FUNDAMENTAL HUMAN
RIGHTS, IN THE DIGNITY AND WORTH OF THE HUMAN
PERSON, IN THE EQUAL RIGHTS OF MEN AND WOMEN
AND OF NATIONS LARGE AND SMALL, AND

TO ESTABLISH CONDITIONS UNDER WHICH JUSTICE
AND RESPECT FOR THE OBLIGATIONS ARISING FROM

[167]

TREATIES AND OTHER SOURCES OF INTERNATIONAL LAW CAN BE MAINTAINED, AND

TO PROMOTE SOCIAL PROGRESS AND BETTER STANDARDS OF LIFE IN LARGER FREEDOM, AND FOR THESE ENDS

TO PRACTISE TOLERANCE AND LIVE TOGETHER IN PEACE WITH ONE ANOTHER AS GOOD NEIGHBORS, AND

TO UNITE OUR STRENGTH TO MAINTAIN INTERNATIONAL PEACE AND SECURITY, AND

TO ENSURE, BY THE ACCEPTANCE OF PRINCIPLES AND THE INSTITUTION OF METHODS, THAT ARMED FORCE SHALL NOT BE USED, SAVE IN THE COMMON INTEREST, AND

TO EMPLOY INTERNATIONAL MACHINERY FOR THE PROMOTION OF THE ECONOMIC AND SOCIAL ADVANCEMENT OF ALL PEOPLES, HAVE RESOLVED TO COMBINE OUR EFFORTS TO ACCOMPLISH THESE AIMS."

In the years since, the United Nations has wrestled with the bitter problems of our time. In America it has been attacked and ridiculed, but it has also been supported by many who believe that it is the one hope for world peace with justice in a time when cities can be wiped out in a few minutes by forces of unlimited destruction. Through the United Nations' many special agencies mutual help has been given all over the world to peoples and nations in need.

The United Nations Charter has its Bill of Rights, endorsed by the General Assembly. It is called The International Bill of Human Rights. Only a few of the member nations have as yet signed its noble clauses.

But it stands waiting for the time when *all* the member nations will sign it. Liberty is used to waiting. It is only eight hundred years since King John so bitterly signed the Magna Charta on that June day at Runnymede. We have come a long way since then.

INDEX

war with John, 65–67
See also Pope Innocent III
Churchill, Winston, 155, 159–
61, 166
Cinque Ports, 55, 126
Colombia, International Conference at, 151
"Common Sense," by Paine, 140
Congress of American Republics, 150
Constitution, of United States, 142–48
Count of Flanders, 75–76, 87–88
Croxton Abbey, 121
Crusade, Third, 24

d'Albiney, William, 110–11
de Braose, William, 63
de Burgh, Hubert, Dover Castle defended by, 116–17, 125
French fleet defeated by, 126–27
as justiciar, 129
de Grey, John, 59
de Mauleton, Savarie, 111
de Quency, Sayer, 85
Declaration of Independence, 138–39, 142–43
Declaration by the United Nations, 166

Devil, in chronicles, 15–16
"Divine right of kings," 132
Dover, 68, 73, 77, 108–09, 116–18, 155
Dover castle, 107, 117, 125–26
Dover harbor, 127
Druid priests, 2
Duke of Austria, 27
Dunkirk, 155

Earl of Gloucester, 51
Earl of Salisbury, 75–76, 87, 89
Eleanor of Aquitaine, 40–41
enforced seclusion of, 21
John spoiled by, 19
rescued by John, 41–42
Emancipation Proclamation, 144
England, assigned to Pope, 73
departure of French invaders, 128–29
German threat in World War II, 155–56
interdict on, 60, 64
invaded by Louis, 116–18
invasion threatened by Philip, 67
twelfth century in, 6–9 *passim*
vassalage in, 6–8
English Channel, 1, 19, 28, 55, 57, 116, 155

and Isabella of Angoulême, 51
and Jews, 63
and Langton, Stephen, *see* Langton, Stephen
Magna Charta granted by, 105
and Marshal, William, *see* Marshal, William
mercenaries hired by, 109–12, 116
mother of, 41–42
nephew of, 42–44
and Pandulph, 66, 69–73
pardoned by Richard, 30
and Philip of France, *see* Philip of France
and Pope, *see* Pope Innocent III
portents believed by, 50
prophecy by Peter of Wakefield, 62, 64, 71, 73
relief at death of Walter, 58
at Runnymede, 104–05
and son Henry, 121
and son Richard, 127
superstitious nature of, 50, 64
temper of, 52–53, 60
treason of, to brother, 28–30
to father, 21
and Walter, Hubert, 38–39, 57–59

Welsh rebels defeated by, 63–64
Jugglers, at feast in castle, 14
Justiciars, 28

King Arthur, legend of, 2
King Charles I, 132
King George III, 132
King Henry I, 83
King Henry II, 19, 21, 80
King Henry III, 124
King James II, 132
King John, *see* John
King Philip, *see* Philip of France
King Richard, *see* Richard
Kings, "divine right of," 132
Knights Templars, 73

La Roche-au-Moine, castle of, 87
Lackland, John, 19
Lambeth, Treaty of, 128–29
Langton, Stephen, Bible read by, 100, 122–23
charter of Henry I found by, 83–84
civil war prevented by, 82
and John, 60, 65, 77–79, 81–82, 85, 91–98, 101, 105, 110
and Pope, 59, 65, 115, 122

return from France, 77, 81
return from Rome, 129
Rochester castle delivered to
    barons, 110
in Rome, 115, 122–23
League of Nations, Covenant
    of, 153–54
Leyden, Holland, 134
Lincoln, Abraham, quotations
    from, 144–45
Lincoln, England, 117, 121, 125
"Lincoln Green, Merry Men
    of," 46–48
Little John, 47–48
Litvinov, Maxim, 166
London, barons in, 109, 111–12,
    117–18
capture by barons, 99
Louis's retreat to, 125
New Temple in, 91
siege by Marshal, 126, 128
Long Beard, William of the, 48
Louis, 87, 109, 113
defeat of, 125, 128–29
England invaded by, 116–18,
    125–26
return to France, 129
Lynn, 118

Magna Charta, 8–9, 104, 123,
    132, 169

annulled by Pope, 114–15, 122
granted by John, 105
provisions of, 106, 130
restored by Henry III, 128
Marshal, William, 26, 92–93, 98,
    100, 121
as guardian of Henry III, 121,
    124, 128–29
and John, 36, 38, 55–57, 92–93,
    98, 100, 105, 121
Louis defeated by, 125, 128
at Runnymede, 105
war with France opposed by,
    55–57
Mayflower, 134–36
Mayflower Compact, 134–37
Merchants, guilds formed by, 49
"Merry Men," 46–48
Minstrel, at feast in castle, 13
Mirebeau, Castle of, 41, 50
Mussolini, and League of Na-
    tions, 154

New Temple, London, 91
Newfoundland, 160
Norfolk, province of, 117
Normandy, 28, 31, 39, 51, 53,
    55
Normans, 2
as builders, 10
characteristics of, 20

[177]